# Gifts to
# make for
# children

M. EVANS AND COMPANY, INC.
New York, New York 10017

**Designers**
Kate Cooper: snake, Punch and Judy,
merry-go-round, Jack-in-the-box
Audrey Vincente Dean: Snakes and ladders,
caterpillar
Jenny Fischer: playhouse
Sylvia Gifford: frog
Anne Griffiths: rag dolls
Eleanor designs: canvas tunnel, hobby horse
Eleanor Harvey: finger puppets
Peggie Hayden: teddy bears, cuddly companions
Audrey Hersch: dolls' house, felt models
Janet Mitchener: Bell nose, patchwork dog
Francis Newell: kite
Margaret Spiers: doll nightie case
Elisabeth Williams: hand puppet


**Pictures supplied by**
Steve Bicknell 49, 62, 63, 66.
John Carter 70.
Alan Duns 36, 43.
Galt Toys 5.
Chris Lewis 8/9, 18, 20, 23, 28, 54, 55.
Sandra Lousada 51.
Julian Nieman 58/59.
Roger Phillips 12, 13, 14/15, 17, 46.
Peter Pugh Cook 24/25, 30, 35, 67.
Rupert Watts 38, 40.

**Key to Symbols**
[    ]    American equivalents
W. S.    Wrong side
R. S.    Right side

**Edited by Sarah Parr**

M. Evans and Company titles are distributed in the United
States by the J. B. Lippincott Company, East Washington
Square, Philadelphia, Pa. 19105

Published in 1976 by M. Evans and Company, New York,
  New York by arrangement with Marshall Cavendish
  Publications Limited, London

ISBN 0-87131-214-X

# Introduction

Finding an individual gift for today's child is no easy task. So here is a collection of super presents that will keep boys and girls occupied for hours. You will have no problem finding the right one—a hobby horse or playhouse is ideal for outdoor lovers with active imaginations, while a puppet or Jack-in-the-box will suit those who prefer quiet indoor play. Those popular companions, teddy bears and soft toys, will always be welcomed too, or you could introduce a child to Bell nose, a tall, friendly character who bounces along on a piece of elastic.

The step-by-step instructions and graph or trace patterns are supplemented by clear diagrams, and each project is well illustrated. All you will need for many of the gifts are bits of fabric and everyday household materials. For the experienced there is ample scope for creating personal colour schemes and finishing touches. The kite, for instance, can be decorated to suit the recipient's taste. So start choosing your first present now from the comfort of your armchair and discover the pleasures of making a special and unusual gift for any occasion.

*Snakes and ladders—a gift that will delight children and keep them happy for hours. Instructions for playing the game and making the board are on page 36.*

# Contents

# Six rag dolls

Here are six small people to sew. This family of rag dolls is made from one basic pattern. The dolls' clothes are simple to make up from the patterns, and they can easily be adapted to suit particular play requirements. Old stockings [hose] or foam pieces could be used instead of kapok for stuffing the dolls.

**For each doll you will need:**
- [ ] 30.5cm by 30.5cm *(12in by 12in)* piece of cotton fabric
- [ ] kapok; glue suitable for fabric
- [ ] embroidery thread in pink and black, for features
- [ ] scraps of left-over fabric, ribbon and braid for clothes
- [ ] narrow elastic
- [ ] hooks and eyes

## To make the doll

Draw up the basic doll pattern pieces from the graph pattern in which one square equals 2.5cm *(1in)*. With right sides together, tack [baste] and stitch the two sections taking 0.6cm *(¼in)* seam allowance and leaving 5cm *(2in)* open at the top of the head for turning and stuffing. Clip curves, turn to the right side. Stuff the doll firmly and oversew [overcast] the opening to close. Work the eyes on each doll in satin stitch, using black embroidery thread. For the girl dolls add stitched eyelashes,

worked above or below the eye. Work a curved line in stem stitch, using pink embroidery thread, to form the mouth of the boy dolls. Work a satin-stitched Cupid's bow in pink embroidery thread for the girl dolls. Use a felt-tipped pen to make freckles and round pink cheeks. To make the hair, use the bobbles [balls] from bobble fringing [ball fringe] stitched firmly in place, or thread a large needle with double knitting wool [yarn] and make large loops all over the head. Alternatively you could take a thick hank of double knitting wool [yarn], back stitch it down the centre to give the effect of a parting, and plait it at either side of the doll's head to the length required.

# To make the clothes

## Girl with black choker

Draw up the dress pattern piece from the graph pattern. Cut out from flowered fabric. Cut one dress piece down the line indicated on the pattern piece. For the sleeve frills, cut two lengths of flowered fabric 18cm by 2.5cm (7in by 1in). With right sides together, stitch the dress side seams. Run a line of gathering stitches down one long side of each sleeve frill, pull up to fit armholes. Tack [baste] and stitch in place. Stitch back seam, leaving open a length long enough for dress to be slipped over doll's head. Stitch a hook and eye at neck edge to close. Turn dress to right side and fit it on doll. Draw up the pants pattern piece and cut it out from white cotton fabric. With right sides together, stitch the pants pieces together across the crotch and down the side seams. Turn the pants to the right side and add a trimming of narrow lace around the legs. Turn a narrow hem at the waist edge and insert a length of elastic. Stitch three small black beads down the front of the dress bodice. Thread beads on strong thread to make a choker. Finish off doll with a bow of black ribbon in her hair.

## Girl with waistcoat [bolero]

Draw up the basic bodice pattern from the graph. Cut out from white cotton fabric. Cut one bodice piece down the line indicated on the pattern. With wrong sides together, stitch the side and sleeve seams. Turn to the right side and add a broderie anglaise trim at neck and cuffs. Stitch a hook and eye at the neck edge to secure. Draw up the basic waistcoat pattern from the graph. Cut out from purple felt.

Cut one waistcoat piece along line indicated on pattern. Stitch shoulder and side seams. Stitch pink braid around waistcoat and sleeve edges.

To make the skirt, cut a piece of flowered fabric 18cm by 2.5cm (7in by 1in) for the waistband, a piece 43cm by 12.5cm (17in by 5in) for the main skirt piece, and a piece 71cm by 2.5cm (28in by 1in) for the frill. Run a line of gathering stitches along one long edge of the frill piece, and pull up to fit the skirt edge. With right sides together, tack [baste] and stitch. Run a line of gathering stitches along the top edge of the skirt and pull up to fit the waistband. With right sides together, tack [baste] and stitch the waistband to the skirt. Fold the waistband over and slip stitch on the wrong side. Stitch the back seam, leaving an opening large enough for the skirt to be fitted on the doll. Stitch a hook and eye in position to close. Put a small artificial flower in hair. Stitch another to waistcoat.

## Girl with mob cap

Cut out the bodice pieces, cutting them short across the dotted line indicated on the pattern. Make up the bodice as above, gathering the sleeves at the wrist edge. Cut a strip of fabric 2.5cm by 51cm (1in by 20in) long and gather one long edge to fit the bodice neck. With right sides together, tack [baste] and stitch in place. Make the frilled skirt as described above, omitting the waistband. With right sides together, tack [baste] and stitch the skirt to the bodice. Stitch a hook and eye at the back neck-opening of the bodice.

To make the mob cap, cut a 14cm (5½in) diameter circle of flowered fabric. Turn a narrow hem around the edge of the circle. Run two rows of gathering elastic [elasticized thread] 2cm (¾in) and 2.5cm (1in) from the edge of circle, and pull up to fit the head. Stitch a large artificial flower on the hat brim and a smaller flower on bodice front.

## Boy in blue suit

Cut out the jacket from the basic bodice pattern and make up in dark blue fabric as described above. Cut a strip of blue fabric 18cm by 2.5cm (7in by 1in) and, wrong sides together, stitch it to the neck edge. Turn the strip over to the wrong side and slip stitch in position to form a stand-up collar. Stitch orange ricrac braid around the neck, cuffs and jacket hem. Cut three small circles of orange felt and stick in position down the front of the jacket to represent buttons. Stitch a hook and eye at the back neck opening to secure. Draw up the basic trouser pattern from the graph, and cut out from the dark blue fabric. Join centre seams and then inside and outside leg seams. Turn a narrow hem at the waist edge and insert elastic. Pull up to fit doll and secure. Stitch orange ricrac around the bottom of each leg to finish off.

## Boy in red suit

Make up the bodice in green fabric, and edge the cuffs with red and green braid. Make up the trousers in red fabric, and add a green buttonhole-stitched patch at the knee. Finish off the doll with a scarf of red ribbon or tape.

## Boy in purple shorts

Make up the bodice in red fabric. Cut the sleeves short, and add buttons cut from green felt. Cut a tiny pocket and stitch in place on the shirt, adding a triangle of green felt for a handkerchief. Make up the shorts in purple fabric, using the basic trousers pattern and cutting the legs short across the dotted line indicated on the pattern. Cut two strips of purple fabric each 10cm by 2.5cm (4in by 1in) Fold in half lengthways and stitch. Stitch the straps to the shorts, positioning them so that they cross over at the back.

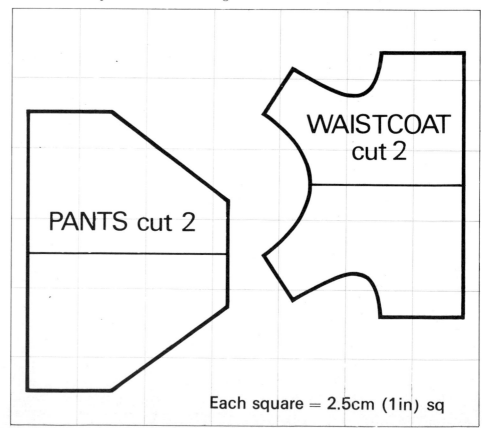

PANTS cut 2

WAISTCOAT cut 2

Each square = 2.5cm (1in) sq

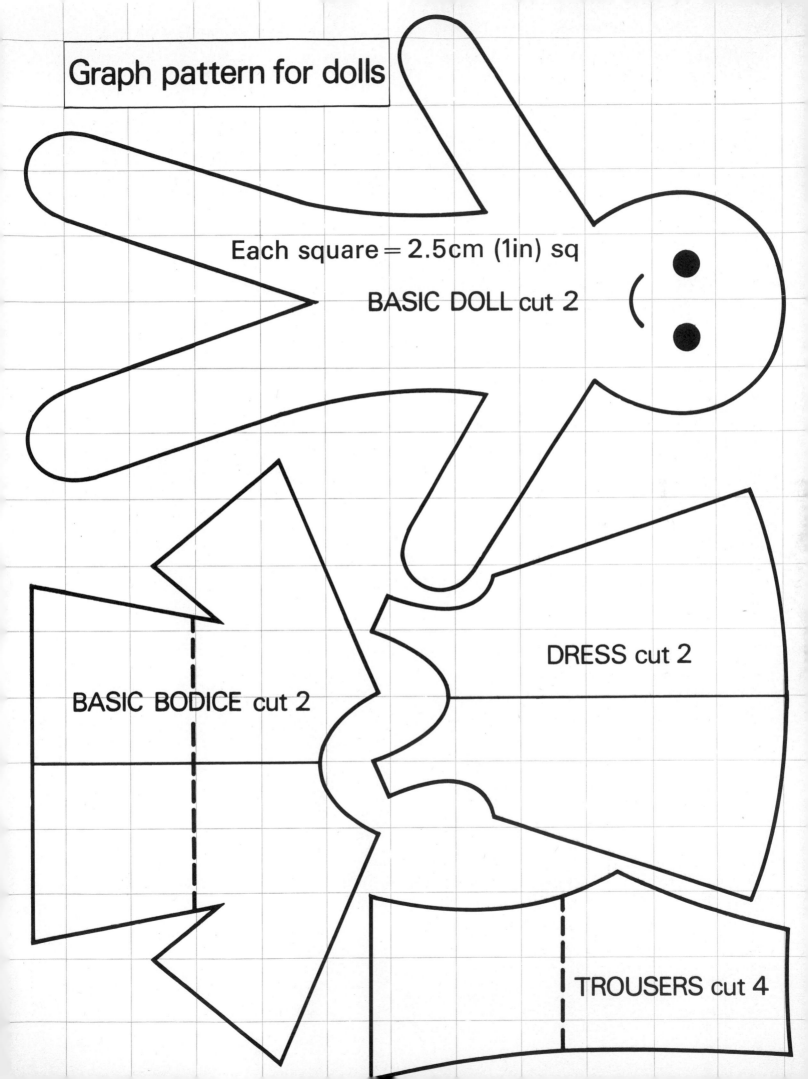

# Graph pattern for dolls

Each square = 2.5cm (1in) sq

BASIC DOLL cut 2

BASIC BODICE cut 2

DRESS cut 2

TROUSERS cut 4

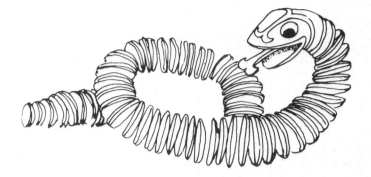

# A friendly snake

This multi-coloured snake is an appealing toy for all ages. The head is worked in felt, while the body is made up of padded discs of fabric threaded onto elastic which makes the snake soft, flexible and safe.

## To make the snake
### You will need:
- [ ] two 30.5cm *(12in)* squares of green felt
- [ ] piece of pink felt measuring 18cm by 35.5cm *(7in by 14in)*
- [ ] piece of yellow felt measuring 25.5cm by 18cm *(10in by 7in)*
- [ ] small pieces of black and white felt
- [ ] 0.9m *(1yd)* 0.6cm *($\frac{1}{4}$in)* wide elastic
- [ ] scraps of colourful lightweight fabric
- [ ] pieces of old blanket
- [ ] kapok or foam rubber chips
- [ ] white embroidery thread
- [ ] sewing thread

### Body
Cut out two circles from fabric and one circle from the blanket for each segment. Place the two fabric circles together with right sides facing and the blanket circle on top. Tack [baste] together and machine stitch with a 0.6cm *($\frac{1}{4}$in)* seam, leaving a 4cm *(1$\frac{1}{2}$in)* opening. Trim seam if necessary, clip, turn and press. Insert a little kapok and slip stitch opening.

You will need 68 circles threaded together in the following order of finished sizes, remembering to allow 1.3cm *($\frac{1}{2}$in)* on each diameter for turnings.

**Neck.** 1x8cm *(3$\frac{1}{4}$in)*, 1x9cm *(3$\frac{1}{2}$in)*, 1x9.5cm *(3$\frac{3}{4}$in)*, 1x10cm *(4in)*, 1x 10.5cm *(4$\frac{1}{4}$in)*, 1x11.5cm *(4$\frac{1}{2}$in)*, 1x 12cm *(4$\frac{3}{4}$in)*.
**Body.** 40x12.5cm *(5in)*.
**Tail.** 2x12cm *(4$\frac{3}{4}$in)*, 2x11.5cm *(4$\frac{1}{2}$in)*, 2x10.5cm *(4$\frac{1}{4}$in)*, 2x10cm *(4in)*, 2x 9.5cm *(3$\frac{3}{4}$in)*, 2x9cm *(3$\frac{1}{2}$in)*, 2x8cm *(3$\frac{1}{4}$in)*, 2x7.5cm *(3in)*, 1x7cm *(2$\frac{3}{4}$in)*, 2x6.5cm *(2$\frac{1}{2}$in)*, 2x5cm *(2in)*.

### Head
Draw up the head and mouthpiece from the graph pattern. Cut out two head pieces from green felt and one mouthpiece from pink felt.
Place the two pieces of green felt together and insert the pink mouthpiece in the front part of the head, placing the fold as shown on graph pattern. Stitch them firmly together with matching thread.
Cut out two tongue pieces from the black felt and stitch firmly together. Embroider the tongue with white running stitch and sew it to the folded mouth section at this stage before completing the head.
Stuff the head section with kapok, inserting more stuffing in the top section than in the bottom section of the jaw, making sure that the stuffing is firm round the neck. To finish the neck, cut out one 8cm *(3$\frac{1}{4}$in)* circle from the green felt and one from the blanket and reinforce on the blanket side with a piece of tape [seam binding] as shown in diagram. Thread about 2.5cm *(1in)* of elastic through to the wrong side and stitch firmly to tape [seam binding]. Complete head by stitching neck end firmly on to head piece.
Cut out two circles of white felt and two smaller circles of black felt for the eyes. Sew the eyes in place, inserting a small amount of kapok under each white circle. Sew or stick the yellow felt decorations onto the head.

### Making up
Thread the rest of the elastic through the centre of the completed discs of fabric, in the order mentioned above, and pull to the desired length. Knot the end firmly and stitch in place. Cover the knot by sewing a felt piece over it on the last tail disc.

# Graph pattern for snake's head

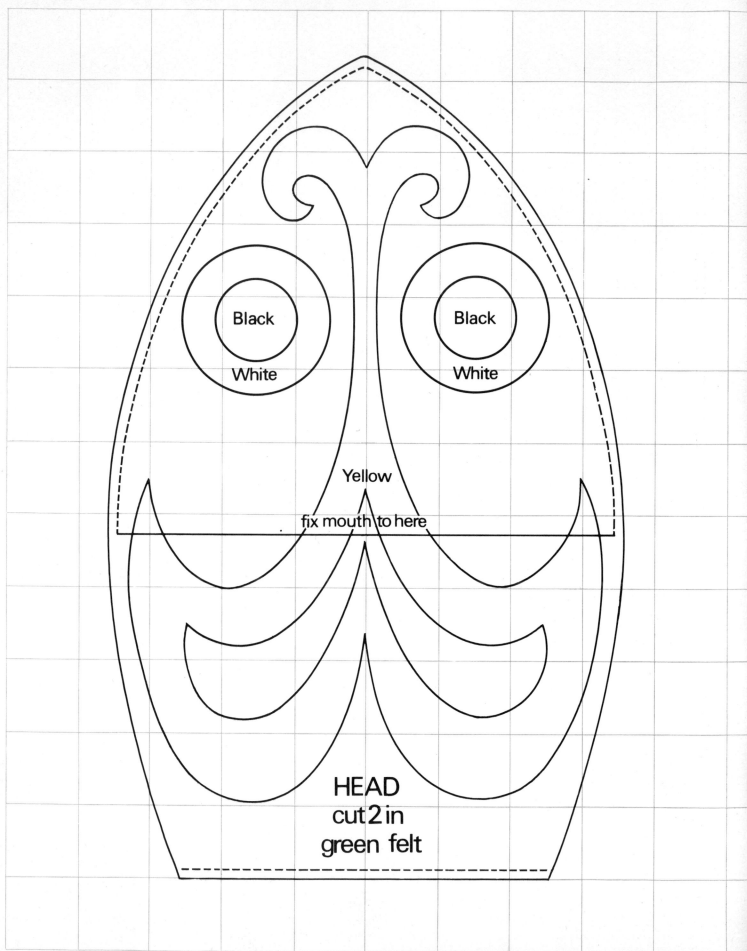

Black

White

Black

White

Yellow

fix mouth to here

HEAD
cut 2 in
green felt

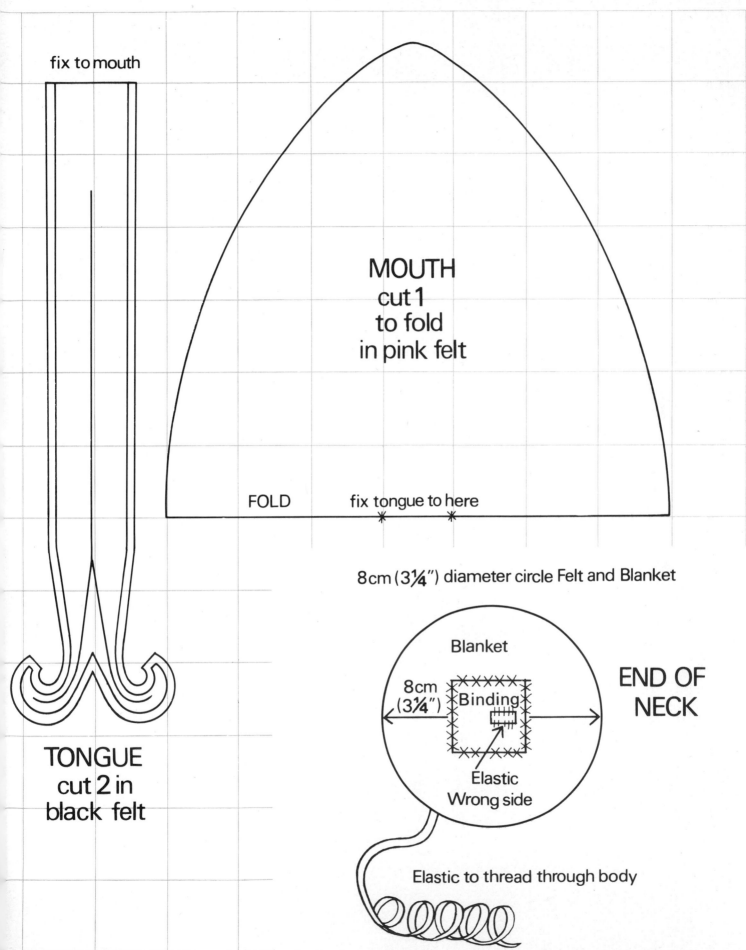

Each square = 2.5cm (1in) sq

fix to mouth

MOUTH
cut 1
to fold
in pink felt

FOLD        fix tongue to here

8cm (3¼") diameter circle Felt and Blanket

Blanket

8cm
(3¼")    Binding

END OF
NECK

Elastic
Wrong side

TONGUE
cut 2 in
black felt

Elastic to thread through body

# Models in felt

Colourful and great fun – these are stuffed toys with a difference. Choose a cheerful yellow car, a splendid red engine or a smart little plane. Made from felt stuffed with kapok, they are chunky yet soft for safe play.

## The plane

**You will need:**

☐ 46cm *(18in)* square of blue felt
☐ scraps of white, yellow, red, black and apricot felt
☐ yellow, black, red and blue soft embroidery thread
☐ 3 pipe cleaners
☐ two 2cm *(¾in)* diameter buttons
☐ one 1.3cm *(½in)* diameter button
☐ kapok or foam rubber chips

**To make the plane**

Draw up the pattern from the squared diagram and cut out two side bodies, four wings and four tail fins.

Pin the two side bodies right sides together and oversew [overcast] all round, leaving a small gap. Turn work to right side and stuff firmly. Close gap. Sew the wings together in pairs right sides together, leaving the straight bases open. Turn the work. Stuff each wing firmly, then sew to the body so that the front seam of each wing is about 2.5cm *(1in)* away from the nose and the under surface is about 2.5cm *(1in)* away from the lower centre seam. Sew and stuff the tail fins similarly and stitch them in place so that the back seam is 2cm *(¾in)* away from the centre seam at the back of the tail fin and the under surface 2.5cm *(1in)* away from the lower centre seam.

**Propeller.** Bend a 20.5cm *(8in)* pipe cleaner in two and cover it with white felt, rounding the ends. Cut another pipe cleaner in half and bend it in two. Cover it with white felt. Bend the longer piece into a V and sew one end of the shorter piece to the point of the V. Stitch the centre of the three blades firmly to the nose of the plane.

Cut a 4.5cm *(1¾in)* diameter circle of white felt and cut out a quarter of the circle. Join the straight edges and turn the seam to the inside. Insert stuffing into this cone and stitch it over the top of the propeller blades, adding more kapok if necessary so that it forms a smooth, neat dome shape.

**Pilot.** Use the trace pattern for the dome of the engine, but trim away 0.6cm *(¼in)* from the straight edge. Cut two pieces of apricot felt and join them round the curved side. Turn the seam to the inside. Stuff the shape and sew it to the top centre, matching front and back seams.

Cut two red helmet sides from the trace pattern and join them round the curved edge. Turn the seam to the inside and slip it onto the head. Cut a strip of white felt 2.5cm by 0.6cm *(1in by ¼in)* and sew it just below the centre front of helmet. Embroider the mouth and eyes, then work black stem stitch round the goggle and helmet edges.

**Wheels.** For each front wheel leg double a 7.5cm *(3in)* length of pipe cleaner and cover it with blue felt. Sew the larger buttons to one side of the legs, then make a slit in the underside of each wing 3.8cm *(1½in)* away from the body and insert the legs so that approximately 2.5cm *(1in)* protrudes and the wheels are towards the inside. For the back wheel cover a 5cm *(2in)* single piece of pipe cleaner with blue felt, bend it in two and sew the smaller button in between the free ends. Cut a slit in the centre lower seam about 2.5cm *(1in)* from the end and insert the pipe cleaner so that about 1.3cm *(½in)* protrudes. Sew the pipe cleaner in place.

**Decorations to plane body.** For the rings on each end of the wings cut a 3.8cm *(1½in)* diameter circle of yellow felt, then cut successively smaller circles of blue, white and red felt. Sew them one on top of the other and stitch to the wings.

Cut two strips of yellow felt each 0.6cm by 12.5cm *(¼in by 5in)* and sew them round the wings to finish next to the wheel legs. Cut a 1cm *(⅜in)* wide strip of black felt and stick it round the plane body to meet at the seam on the underside.

For each tail fin decoration cut a 2.5cm *(1in)* square of yellow felt and pieces of red and white felt each 2.5cm by 0.6cm *(1in by ¼in)*. Sew them on top of the yellow felt and stitch to each side of the tail.

Work black stem stitch round the propeller and the pilot, and black running stitch round the yellow strips on the wings. Work yellow running stitch round the pilot and round the black body strip.

## The engine

**You will need:**

☐ 46cm *(18in)* square of red felt
☐ 30.5cm *(12in)* square of grey felt
☐ scraps of yellow, blue, mustard, black, apricot and white felt
☐ 6 black buttons 2cm *(¾in)* diameter
☐ 2 pipe cleaners
☐ piece of thin dowel or short pencil 7.5cm *(3in)* long
☐ black, yellow, red, blue and brown soft embroidery thread
☐ glue suitable for fabric
☐ black felt tip pen
☐ kapok or foam rubber chips

**To make the engine**

**Engine body.** Draw up the pattern from the squared diagram and cut two cab sides from the red felt and two lower engine sides from the grey felt. Cut and piece one red gusset 50cm by 9cm *(19½in by 3½in)* and one grey gusset 32cm by 9cm *(12½in by 3½in)*. Sew the lower edge of each cab A – B to the upper straight edge of the lower engine bodies A – B. Oversew [overcast] one short end of each red and grey gusset together. With the seam to the

*Detail of the engine back.*

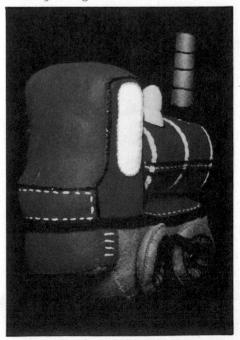

outside, pin one outer edge to the corner C of the lower engine body.

Pin and oversew [overcast] the rest of the red gusset to the engine body so that it ends at the front corner D. Pin and oversew [overcast] the grey gusset to the lower engine body so that it meets the free end of the red gusset.

Turn the work to the right side. Stuff firmly, then close the opening.

**Wheels.** Cut eight circles 7.5cm *(3in)* in diameter from grey felt. Cut a circle 5cm *(2in)* in diameter from thin card and place it centrally on one of the grey circles. Mark round it lightly with a black felt tip pen. Repeat with three other circles.

Work stem stitch in black round the felt tip lines, then lay eight straight stitches across the worked circle so that there are sixteen stitches radiating from the centre to represent spokes. Secure the stitches by one or two oversewing [overcasting] stitches over the centre.

Oversew [overcast] the embroidered wheels to the plain ones and stuff lightly. Attach the wheels to the engine body with buttons as described for the car. Cover two 10cm *(4in)* lengths of pipe cleaner with black felt and oversew [overcast] the edges, then stitch them to connect the pairs of wheels as shown in the illustration.

**Boiler.** From red felt cut two 7.5cm *(3in)* circles and a straight strip 12.5cm by 38cm *(5in by 15in)*. Using the trace pattern cut out two domes from yellow felt. Cut one dome edge from yellow felt and one identical funnel edge from black felt.

Oversew [overcast] the short edges of the red straight strip together, leaving a short length in the middle unstitched for stuffing. With the seam to the outside, oversew [overcast] the long edges to the circular pieces of red felt. Turn the work to the right side. Stuff through the opening, then close it.

For the funnel, cut a strip of grey felt 8cm *(3¼in)* wide and roll it round the dowel until the diameter of the roll is 2cm *(¾in)*. Oversew [overcast] the edge. Cut a strip of black felt 0.6cm *(¼in)* wide and roll it round the top of the funnel. Stick or stitch in place.

Embroider four rings of black stem stitch round the funnel, the last 1.3cm *(½in)* above the free end. Wrap the shaped funnel edge round this end just below the last stem stitch ring and stitch in place. Oversew [overcast] the short ends. Insert padding into the funnel edge and sew to the front end of the boiler.

Oversew [overcast] round the curved edges of the dome and turn the seam to the inside. Stuff, then wrap the dome

edge around it, insert padding and sew to the other end of the boiler.

Cut three 0.6cm *(¼in)* strips of yellow felt and stitch them round the boiler, one at the circular seam at either end and the other round the middle. Work black stem stitch and yellow running stitch along the sides of the boiler and around the front as shown in the illustration.

**Windows.** For the side windows, cut two pieces of white felt each 7.5cm by 3.2cm *(3in by 1¼in)* and round off the corners. Cut out a front window the same. Stitch two windows vertically to the cab sides. From the trace pattern, cut out the pieces for the driver and assemble on the left-hand window, placing the blue jacket over the mustard body. Embroider mouth, eyes and neckerchief, and work French knots for hair.

Sew the front window to the upper front of the cab. For the driver's face cut a circle 2cm *(¾in)* in diameter. For his cap cut a pointed oval 2cm by 1.3cm *(¾in by ½in)* and sew it over the top of the circle. Embroider eyes and mouth. Work yellow stem stitch round the windows.

**Stitchery on cab.** Work black stem stitch round the sides of the cab and across the back from E to E. Work yellow running stitch all round the flat part of the engine body where the boiler is to rest, starting and finishing at the front of the cab. Work yellow running stitch also at the curved back of the cab. For the steps, cut two strips of red felt each 2cm by 3.8cm *(¾in by 1½in)*. Sew them under the back lower edges of the cab and work horizontal straight stitches in yellow on them.

**Buffers.** Cut two doubled pieces of pipe cleaner each 2.5cm *(1in)* long and cover them with black felt. Stitch a button to one end of each and wind the thread several times round the pipe cleaners where they are attached to the buttons. At the front end of the train cut two small slits in the grey felt approximately 2cm *(¾in)* down from the join of the gussets and 2cm *(¾in)* in from the sides, and insert the ends of each pipe cleaner. Stitch firmly in place. Cut a 1.3cm *(½in)* strip of black felt long enough to encircle the engine body horizontally and stitch in place as shown in the illustration.

Place the boiler in position, stick down and add stitches to strengthen.

## The car

### You will need:

- [ ] 46cm *(18in)* square of yellow felt
- [ ] 23cm *(9in)* square of white felt
- [ ] 30.5cm *(12in)* square of grey felt
- [ ] scraps of orange, black, blue and apricot felt
- [ ] 6 pipe cleaners
- [ ] 6 white buttons 1.3cm *(½in)* diameter
- [ ] soft embroidery thread in grey, black, white, yellow, red and blue
- [ ] an extra long darning needle
- [ ] one 2cm *(¾in)* diameter curtain ring
- [ ] glue suitable for fabric
- [ ] kapok or foam rubber chips

**To make the car**

**Car body.** Draw up the pattern for the car side from the squared diagram. The positions of the windows are shown by dotted lines and are not to be cut out.

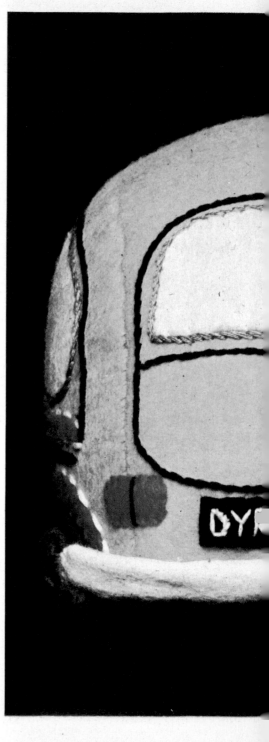

Cut two car sides from the yellow felt and one yellow gusset 39.5cm by 9cm (15½in by 3½in). Cut one grey gusset 30cm by 9cm (11¾in by 3½in). Seam one short end of the yellow and grey gusset together.

With the seam to the outside, pin it at one outer edge to point A on one car side. Pin the rest of the yellow gusset to the upper edge of the car so that it ends at point B.

Pin the grey gusset to the lower edge of the car so that it meets the other short end of the yellow gusset at point B. Oversew [overcast] round the pinned edges but leave the unseamed short edges of the gussets open for stuffing.

Stitch the other sides of the gussets

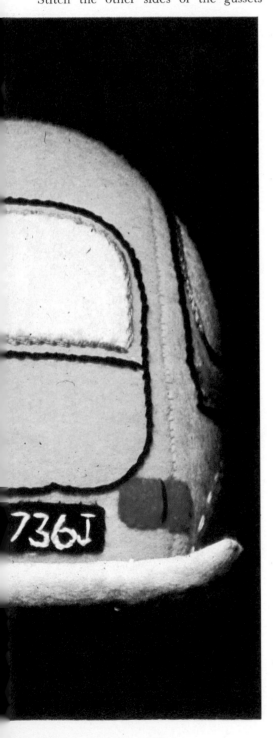

to the car in the same way. Turn the work to the right side. Stuff firmly through the opening, then sew it up.

**Wheels.** Cut eight 5cm (2in) diameter circles from grey felt. Cut four 3.2cm (1¼in) diameter circles from white felt. Pin each white circle centrally to a grey one and oversew [overcast] in position. With wrong sides facing, pin the grey circles together in pairs and oversew [overcast] round each pair. Leave a small opening to stuff each wheel lightly, then close them. Pin a pair of wheels in place on each side of the car. Push the extra long darning needle and strong grey thread through one hole of a button and the centre of one wheel. Continue to push the needle right through the toy to emerge at the centre of the other wheel.

Thread a second button through one hole, come back through other hole and again pierce the toy in the opposite direction to emerge through the second hole of the first button (Fig.1). Tie a firm knot and cut off surplus thread. Attach the other pair of wheels in same way.

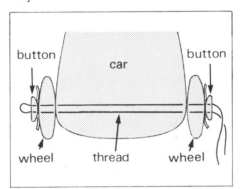

*Fig. 1 Attaching the wheels to the car body with a long darning needle.*

**Windows.** Using the trace pattern, cut from the white felt the front and back windows, two front side windows and two back side windows. Oversew [overcast] the side windows in place as indicated on the graph pattern. Oversew [overcast] the front and back windows in the appropriate positions.

Cut a front and side view driver and passenger from the trace pattern, using apricot felt for the faces and blue and orange for the bodies. Stitch in place. Embroider features using straight stitches or French knots for the hair. Cut a 2cm (¾in) slit in front of the driver at the left or right of the front window to insert the steering wheel. Push half the curtain ring down into the slit and catch the slit together around it. Work buttonhole stitch in black around the ring and add two straight stitches radiating from the centre. Work stem stitch in grey around each window.

**Radiator.** Cut a grey felt radiator from trace pattern and oversew [overcast] in position at the front of the car. Work black vertical straight stitches over it and black stem stitch around it.

**Headlights.** Cut two 2.5cm (1in) circles from black felt and two 2cm (¾in) diameter circles from white felt. Stitch the white circles to the black ones and sew a button in the centre. Oversew [overcast] the assembled lights to the front of the car over the gusset seams.

**Mudguards and side trim.** For the side trim cut two strips of orange felt each 19.5cm (7½in) long by 1cm (⅜in) wide. Taper both ends. Oversew [overcast] in position under the side windows. For the front mudguards cut and stitch down two orange strips each 7.5cm (3in) long by 1cm (⅜in) wide. The front short end touches corner A of the side and the rest of the strip forms a curve above the wheel.

For the back mudguards cut two orange strips each 10cm (4in) long by 1cm (⅜in) wide. Oversew [overcast] in place with the short edges touching the lower edge of the car side. Work white and black running stitches round the mudguards and trims as shown in the illustration.

**Bumpers, number [licence] plates and indicators [turn signals].** For each bumper cut three lengths of pipecleaner each 12.5cm (5in) long and apply glue lightly along the lengths. Lay them side by side on white felt and fold the felt over to enclose them. Trim off the felt around the pipecleaners and oversew [overcast] the edges together. Stick the bumpers centrally to the lower edges of the yellow gusset at the front and back and add a few stitches to strengthen. Bend the ends of the pipe cleaner towards the car body in a curve.

For each number [licence] plate cut a piece of black felt 4.5cm by 1.3cm (1¾in by ½in) and embroider numerals on it in white. Sew the rear number [licence] plate above the bumper and the front one centrally to the front bumper.

The indicators [turn signals] are four pieces of orange felt each 1.3cm by 1.5cm (½in by ⅝in). Sew them to the back and front of the car above the bumpers at each side and make two or three vertical stitches centrally over each.

**Doors and boot [trunk] markings.** Embroider markings on the front, sides and back of the car in black stem stitch following the illustrations.

# Graph pattern for basic model shapes

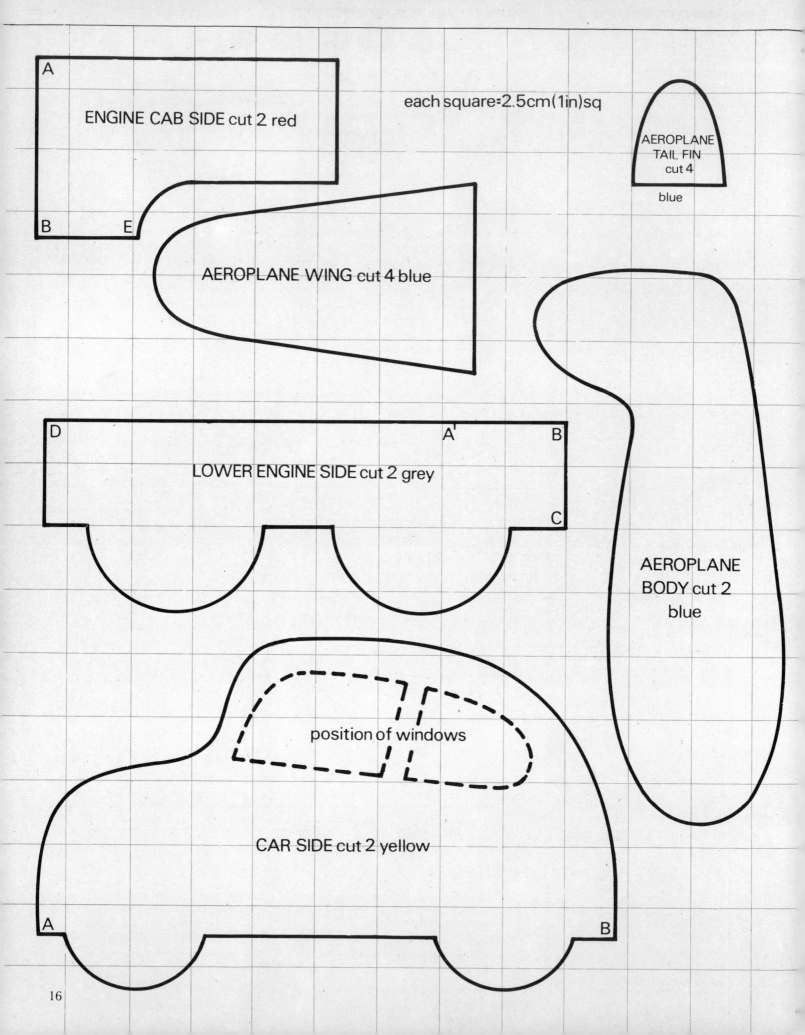

each square=2.5cm(1in)sq

A
ENGINE CAB SIDE cut 2 red
B   E

AEROPLANE TAIL FIN cut 4
blue

AEROPLANE WING cut 4 blue

D          A'          B
LOWER ENGINE SIDE cut 2 grey
C

AEROPLANE BODY cut 2 blue

position of windows

CAR SIDE cut 2 yellow

A                          B

16

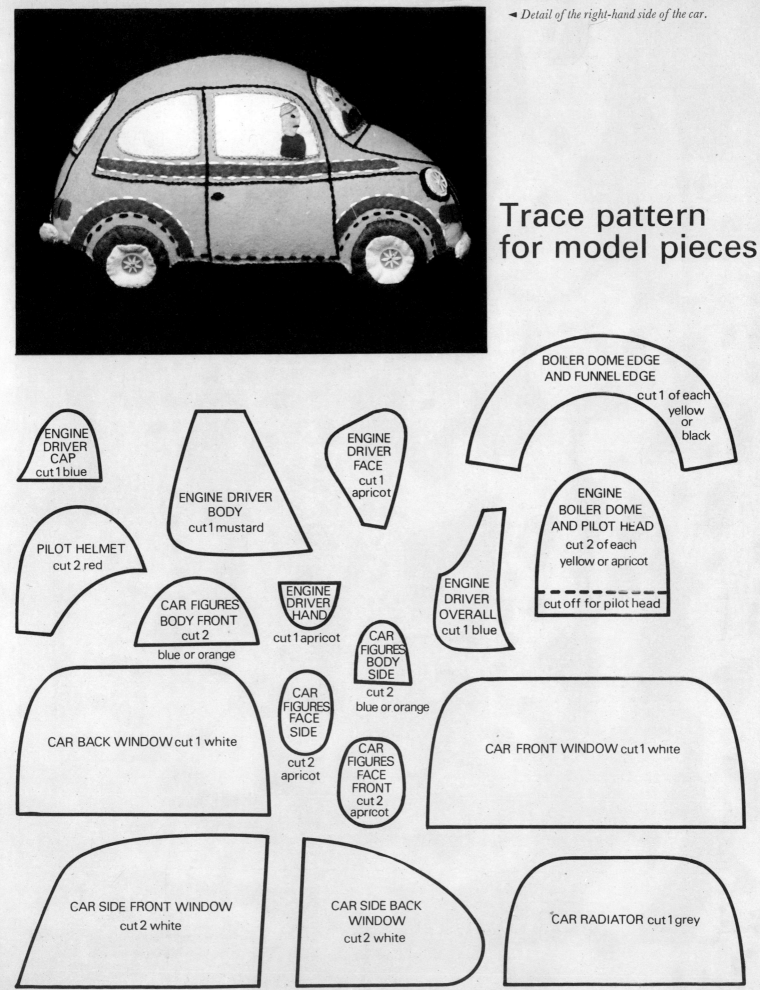

# Trace pattern for model pieces

BOILER DOME EDGE
AND FUNNEL EDGE

cut 1 of each
yellow
or
black

ENGINE
DRIVER
CAP
cut 1 blue

ENGINE DRIVER
BODY
cut 1 mustard

ENGINE
DRIVER
FACE
cut 1
apricot

ENGINE
BOILER DOME
AND PILOT HEAD
cut 2 of each
yellow or apricot

cut off for pilot head

PILOT HELMET
cut 2 red

CAR FIGURES
BODY FRONT
cut 2

blue or orange

ENGINE
DRIVER
HAND

cut 1 apricot

ENGINE
DRIVER
OVERALL
cut 1 blue

CAR
FIGURES
BODY
SIDE

cut 2
blue or orange

CAR
FIGURES
FACE
SIDE

cut 2
apricot

CAR BACK WINDOW cut 1 white

CAR
FIGURES
FACE
FRONT
cut 2
apricot

CAR FRONT WINDOW cut 1 white

CAR SIDE FRONT WINDOW
cut 2 white

CAR SIDE BACK
WINDOW
cut 2 white

CAR RADIATOR cut 1 grey

17

# A patchwork dog

This colourful, soft patchwork dog is easy to sew, and makes a safe and engaging toy for small children. Made up in bright cotton fabrics, Patch is the perfect way to use up left-over scraps of material.

## You will need:

☐ 0.9m *(1yd)* cotton fabric, or scraps of different coloured fabrics
☐ kapok or foam rubber chips
☐ 2 small black buttons, for eyes
☐ black double knitting wool [yarn]
☐ 20.5cm *(8in)* ribbon; a small bell

## To make the dog

Draw up the pattern pieces from the graph pattern. A 1·3cm (½in) seam allowance is given throughout.

Cut one piece A, then reverse the pattern piece to cut the second. Repeat with pattern piece B, using contrast fabric if desired. Cut one piece C, using a third contrast fabric if desired. With right sides together, join both A pieces together from X to Z and both B pieces together from X to W along dotted lines. With right sides together, join the two halves of dog along dotted line between X and Y to form upper body. Pin out the upper body flat with right side uppermost and place piece C on top, right side down.

Matching up leg pieces all round, and working away from point Y, tack [baste] and stitch all round the under body, legs and feet (Fig.1) to join the under part of the dog to the upper body. Leave a small length of seam open for turning and stuffing. Turn dog right side out.

Stuff the body firmly with kapok. Oversew [overcast] the seam to close. Using pattern piece D, cut out four ears from contrasting fabrics, reversing the pattern piece for the second pair. With right sides together, sew each pair of ear shapes together, leaving the straight edges open. Turn right side out. Turn in raw edges of the ears and stitch together, taking a 0.6cm *(¼in)* tuck at right angles to the centre of seam (Fig.2). Stitch the ears to the sides of the head. The tucks hold the ears slightly away from the side of the head.

## To finish the dog

Stitch buttons in position to form the eyes, and use wool [yarn] to work a nose in satin stitch and a mouth in chain stitch (Fig. 3).

Stitch the ribbon around the neck of the dog to form a collar, and stitch the bell to the front of the ribbon.

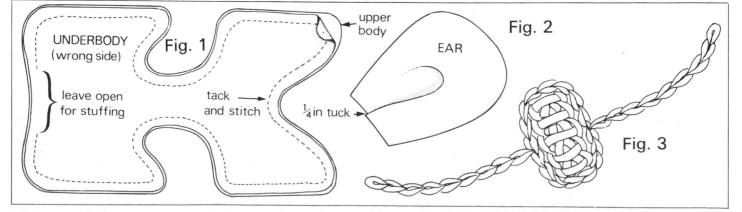

UNDERBODY (wrong side)

leave open for stuffing

Fig. 1

tack and stitch

upper body

EAR

¼ in tuck

Fig. 2

Fig. 3

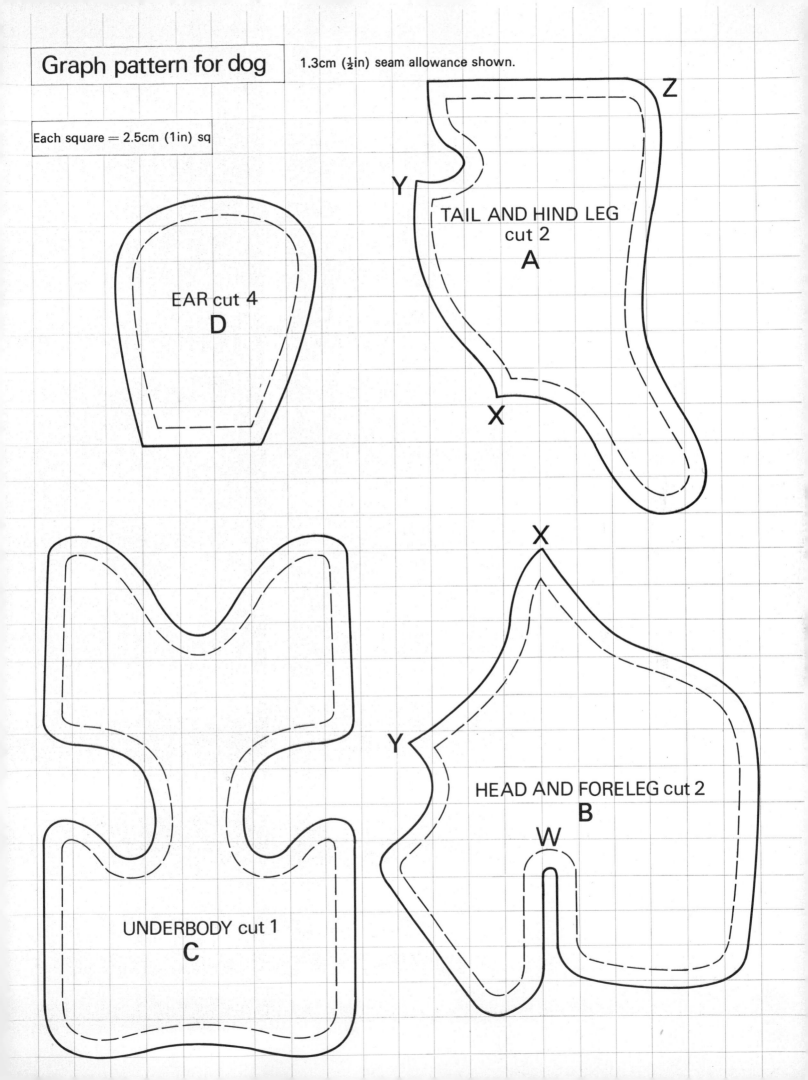

# Graph pattern for dog

1.3cm (½in) seam allowance shown.

Each square = 2.5cm (1in) sq

EAR cut 4
D

TAIL AND HIND LEG
cut 2
A

Y

X

Z

X

Y

HEAD AND FORELEG cut 2
B

W

UNDERBODY cut 1
C

# Giant caterpillar

This appealing caterpillar is designed as an unusual toy or mascot for children of all ages, but it can also double as a sturdy playroom seat. The materials used for making the caterpillar are cheap and easy to buy, and it is made in such a way that it will stand up well to the wear and tear of play.

## To make the caterpillar

### You will need:

- [ ] 0.9m *(1yd)* pink felt
- [ ] 0.25m *(¼yd)* purple felt
- [ ] 1.20m *(1¼yd)* lime green fabric, 90cm *(36in)* wide
- [ ] 2.75m *(3yd)* emerald green fabric, 90cm *(36in)* wide
- [ ] 3 lengths of 2.5cm *(1in)* thick foam rubber, each 1.85m *(6ft)* long by 46cm *(18in)* wide (these lengths may be made up from shorter lengths)
- [ ] two 46cm *(18in)* squares 2.5cm *(1in)* thick foam rubber
- [ ] foam rubber scraps
- [ ] one 46cm *(18in)* diameter foam rubber cushion form (or cut a circle from 7.5cm *(3in)* thick foam)
- [ ] two 76cm *(30in)* cardboard mailing tubes, inside diameter 5cm *(2in)*
- [ ] glue suitable for fabric
- [ ] old newspaper
- [ ] string
- [ ] cardboard
- [ ] 12.5cm *(5in)* length of dowelling
- [ ] toymaker's needle or carpet needle
- [ ] 2 skeins emerald green embroidery thread

### To prepare the stuffing

Cut each 1.85m *(6ft)* length of foam in half lengthways. Cut the mailing tubes into 23cm *(9in)* lengths. Smear glue down one side of a piece of tube and place it over the short end of one foam length. Roll the rubber, without compressing it, round the tube. The circumference of the roll when fully wound should be about 73.5cm *(29in)* and the diameter about 24.5cm *(9½in)*. Tie a length of string round the middle of the roll. Grip the roll firmly between your knees, compressing it as much as possible, and tie a string round each end, about 1.3cm *(½in)* from the edge (Fig.1). Smear each end of the inside of the mailing tube with glue and stuff it loosely with crumpled newspaper. Treat all the rolls except one in the same way. The exception will form the neck and should not be stuffed with

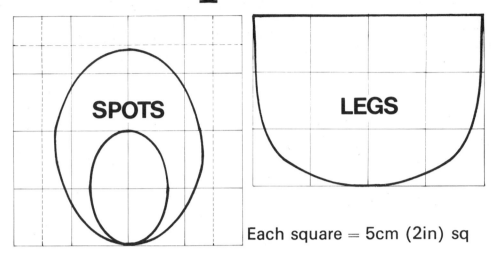

**SPOTS**

**LEGS**

Each square = 5cm (2in) sq

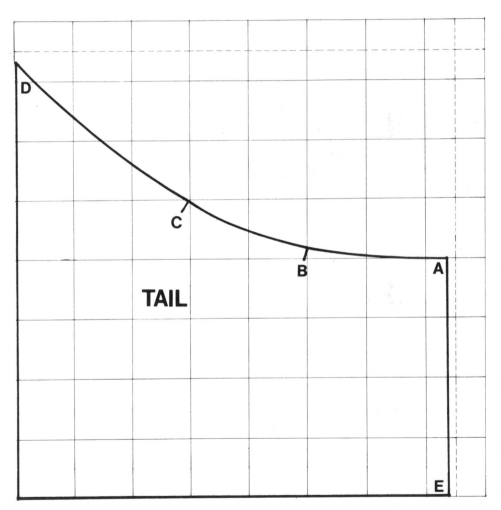

D

C

B　A

TAIL

E

newspaper. To attach the cushion which forms the head to the neck, cut a piece of card 7.5cm *(3in)* square and a length of string about 61cm *(24in)* long. Thread one end of the string into the toymaker's or carpet needle and push it through the circular cushion about 15cm *(6in)* from the edge, then push it through the card square. Take the needle back through

the card about 3.8cm *(1½in)* away from the first hole and push it back through the cushion. Pull the ends of the string level and push them through the mailing tube without the newspaper stuffing. Cut nicks across the centre of the length of dowel and knot the ends of string around it, pulling them up as tightly as possible (Fig.2). Cut a piece of foam and stick it over the depression made in the front of the cushion. Cut a 38cm *(15in)* diameter circle of 2.5cm *(1in)* thick foam and stick it to the front of the cushion.

## To make the body

Draw up the pattern pieces for the tail, legs and spots from the graph pattern given here in which one square equals 5cm *(2in)*. A 1.3cm *(½in)* seam allowance is given throughout, unless otherwise stated. Cut two tail pieces, remembering to reverse the pattern piece if necessary, and 12 legs in emerald green fabric; 12 legs in pink felt; 12 larger spots in pink felt and 12 smaller spots in purple felt.

To make the legs, place a green leg piece to a pink leg piece, right sides together, and stitch. Leave the straight edge open. Turn to the right side and stuff loosely with foam pieces. Oversew [overcast] the raw edges together and repeat for the remaining 11 legs.

For the underbody, cut two pieces from the lime green fabric each measuring 40.5cm *(16in)* by 96.5cm *(38in)*. Join two short edges. For the top body, cut two pieces from the emerald green fabric, one 40.5cm *(16in)* by 96.5cm *(38in)* and one 40.5cm *(16in)* by 61cm *(24in)*. Join two short edges. With right sides together, join the two tail pieces along the curved edges A–B and C–D. B–C is left open for stuffing. Open the tail out flat and join the straight edge E–A–E to the short edge of the shorter upper body piece.

To make the segments, measure 10cm *(4in)* away from the tail seam along the top body. Mark this point at either edge of the fabric with a large tacking [basting] stitch.

Make two more tacking [basting] stitches 20.5cm *(8in)* away from the first pair. Make 8 more sets of marker stitches at intervals of 10cm *(4in)* and 20.5cm *(8in)* alternately (Fig.3). Tack [baste] and stitch a pair of pink spots on each 20.5cm *(8in)* segment, positioning the spots at a slant. Stitch the smaller purple spots on top of the pink ones. The last pair of spots is positioned on the tail 2.5cm *(1in)* away from the tail seam. With the green side of each leg facing the right side of every 20.5cm *(8in)* segment, tack [baste] the straight edges to the sides of each segment. The last pair of legs is tacked to the tail under the spots. Place the right side of the underbody to the right side of the top body, with the legs sandwiched in between. Match the underbody seam to the top body seam. Tack [baste] and stitch the long straight edges together. Fold the top body along the upper seam of the tail and tack [baste] the

edges together from the tail tip D to the point where the top body joins the underbody. Continue tacking [basting] the edges of the underbody together, but increase the seam allowance so that at the lower edge it measures 3.8cm *(1½in)* (Fig.4). Machine stitch, trim away the excess seam allowance and turn the body to the right side.

To gather each segment, thread a sewing needle with 91.5cm *(36in)* of double embroidery thread. Starting at the centre of the top body on the tail seam, make large, even running stitches along the join, across the underbody and back over the top body to the starting point. A chalk line may be

drawn across the underbody for guidance. Stitch around every segment in the same way. There will be 11 gathering lines in all.

## To stuff the body

Push one of the foam rubber rolls down to the tail. Position the end of the roll under the first row of gathering, and pull up the threads firmly around it. The easiest way to do this is to place the toy on the floor and press down with one foot on the foam to compress it. Grip the gathering threads and pull up. Tie in a firm knot and darn the end to secure. Run a gathering thread around the end seam on the underbody

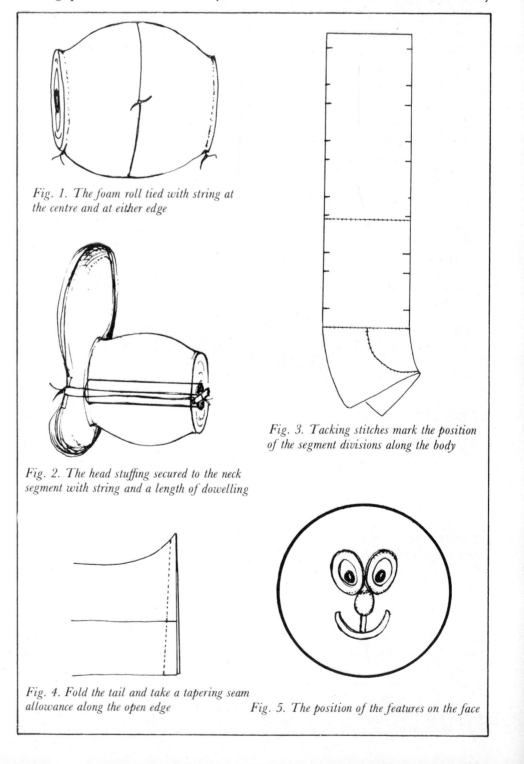

Fig. 1. The foam roll tied with string at the centre and at either edge

Fig. 2. The head stuffing secured to the neck segment with string and a length of dowelling

Fig. 3. Tacking stitches mark the position of the segment divisions along the body

Fig. 4. Fold the tail and take a tapering seam allowance along the open edge

Fig. 5. The position of the features on the face

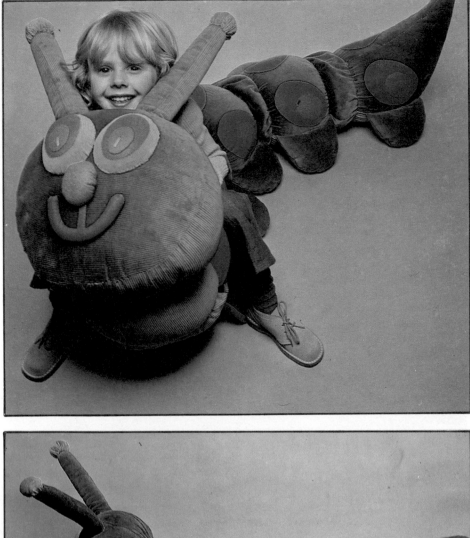

eyes. Run a gathering thread round the edge of the purple felt oval and pull it up to enclose and compress the nose foam.

For the mouth, cut a length of 2.5cm *(1in)* thick foam 20.5cm *(8in)* long by 1.3cm *(½in)* wide. Cut a piece of pink felt 5cm *(2in)* by 21.8cm *(8½in)*. Oversew [overcast] the long edges together round the foam and gather the short edges. Run a gathering thread along one long edge of the felt and pull it up to curve the strip into a smiling mouth. Cut a piece of pink felt 1.3cm *(½in)* wide by 6.5cm *(2½in)* long for the upper lip. To assemble the face (Fig.5) find the centre of the emerald green circle. Then glue the nose with the top of the oval just below the centre. Glue the eyes, just touching each other, above the nose. The upper lip is overlapped by the nose for 1.3cm *(½in)* and the mouth is placed to overlap the lower end of the upper lip by 1.3cm *(½in)*, so that the upper lip measures 3.8cm *(1½in)*. Sew all the features in place from the back of the fabric.

### To join the head to the body

For the back of the head, join pieces of emerald green fabric to give a strip 127cm *(50in)* by 25.5cm *(10in)* wide. Fold it in half with the short edges together and cut along one edge of the material so that the width tapers evenly from 25.5cm *(10in)* in the centre to 15cm *(6in)* on either side. Join the short edge with right sides together. Stitch the face to the long straight edge. Run a gathering thread round the tapered edge. Pull the head over the cushion and foam circle from the front and pull up the gathering thread as tightly as possible. Using the toymaker's or carpet needle and embroidery thread, sew the head firmly to the neck.

### Antennae

Cut two lengths of 2.5cm *(1in)* thick foam each 20.5cm *(8in)* by 28cm *(11in)*. Roll each up lengthways, and bind with embroidery thread to secure. Cut two pieces of emerald green fabric 23cm *(9in)* by 28cm *(11in)*. Turn in one long raw edge 2cm *(¾in)* and sew the fabric strip around the foam, overlapping the long edges rather more at one end to give a tapered shape.

For the knobs at the end of the antennae, cut two circles of lime green fabric each 12.5cm *(5in)* in diameter. Run a gathering thread round the outer edges. Stuff the circle with loose foam and pull up the gathering threads. Sew one knob to the tapered end of each antenna. Stitch the antennae firmly in position to the top of the head.

---

section of the tail and pull up tightly. Stuff tail through opening B–C and oversew [overcast] to close.

Put six handfuls of foam rubber chips on top of the foam rubber roll to pad the next segment slightly without reducing the toy's flexibility, then push the next roll into place. Pull up the gathering threads in the same way to enclose the ends. Continue to stuff along the body in the same way, alternating loose stuffing with foam rolls. Put the neck roll into the last segment and push the excess body fabric between the neck and the head.

### The head

**The face.** Cut a 40.5cm *(16in)* diameter circle of emerald green fabric. For the eyes, cut two cardboard ovals each 12.5cm *(5in)* long by 9cm *(3½in)*

across the widest part. Glue a layer of 2.5cm *(1in)* thick foam rubber on one side. Cut two ovals of lime green fabric each about 3.8cm *(1½in)* larger all round than the cardboard ovals. Run a gathering thread round the outer edge. Place the wrong side to the foam padding on the card and draw up the gathering thread. Stick the excess material to the wrong side of the cardboard. Cut two ovals of pink felt 10cm *(4in)* long by 6.5cm *(2½in)* across the widest part and sew them to the centres of the lime green eyes. Cut two purple ovals 5cm *(2in)* long by 3.8cm *(1½in)* wide and sew them to the lower part of the pink ovals. For the nose, cut a purple felt oval the same size as the cardboard ovals used for the eyes. Cut a piece of 2.5cm *(1in)* thick foam to the same size as the pink ovals used for the

# Merry-go-round

Here's a delightful toy merry-go-round that's great fun to play with. Make the horses spin round by simply turning the knob on top of the canopy. With this gift too you can choose your own colour schemes, decorations and finishing touches.

## To make the merry-go-round

### You will need:
- [ ] a cake base approximately 25.5cm (10in) diameter
- [ ] cardboard tube approximately 18cm (7in) long and 5cm (2in) diameter
- [ ] strong cardboard
- [ ] circular metal sticking plaster [adhesive tape] reel to fit inside tube (see Fig.1)
- [ ] wooden dowel 30.5cm (12in) long and 1cm ($\frac{3}{8}$in) diameter
- [ ] small wooden ball
- [ ] strong glue
- [ ] pieces of felt for horses and base and scraps of felt for decoration
- [ ] cotton fabric for canopy roof
- [ ] matching thread
- [ ] white wool [yarn] for manes and tails
- [ ] 8 small black beads
- [ ] stuffing for horses
- [ ] sharp-bladed handyman's knife

### Base
Cover the surface of the cake base with a circle of felt and cover the edge in a contrasting colour. Decorate the surface with different coloured felt shapes cut from the trace pattern, and the edge with a row of scallops.

### Canopy roof
Using the trace pattern, cut eight triangles with flaps from strong cardboard. Bend the flaps inwards and glue the triangles together to form a pointed roof. Cut off the tip of the roof to allow the dowel to pass through.
Cut eight triangles from patterned cotton fabric, or four from one fabric and four from another as shown here, allowing 0.6cm ($\frac{1}{4}$in) all round for turning [seam allowance]. Stitch them together, leaving a small opening at the tip as shown on the trace pattern, to form a cover for the roof. Glue in place over the cardboard roof.

### Underside of canopy
To form the underside of the canopy, draw a regular octagon on cardboard with 12cm (4$\frac{3}{4}$in) sides and angles of 135 degrees. Cut out and make a small hole in the centre through which the dowel can pass.

### Canopy edge
Cut a strip of cardboard 7.5cm (3in) wide and just over 97cm (38$\frac{1}{4}$in) long. Score it, with a handyman's knife, at 12cm (4$\frac{3}{4}$in) intervals and also 0.6cm ($\frac{1}{4}$in) in from one long side and one short side so that the cardboard can be bent into shape. Cut a zig-zag edge along one side and a series of flaps along the other (see trace pattern).
Cover the strip with felt cut to the same shape, bend it into an octagon and glue to hold. Bend the flaps towards the centre, place over the underside of the canopy so that the eight sides line up and glue down. Decorate the edge with two strips of felt, one plain and one cut into scallops, and stick eight circular motifs over the top as shown in the illustration.

### Central column
To make the central support for the merry-go-round, cover the cardboard tube with a rectangle of felt measuring 19.5cm (7$\frac{1}{2}$in) by 15.5cm (6$\frac{1}{4}$in).

### Horses
For each horse cut from brown felt two body pieces, two ears and a gusset strip 1.3cm ($\frac{1}{2}$in) wide to go around the body shape. Stitch pieces firmly together, leaving a gap for stuffing before completing the stitching.
Attach two small black beads for eyes. Bend a pipe cleaner and sew to the horse's back, then make a decorative saddle and sew in place over pipe cleaner. Make mane and tail from white wool [yarn] and stitch securely in position.
Cover the pipe cleaner by winding strips of felt round it. Insert 1.3cm ($\frac{1}{2}$in) of the end of the cleaner through the canopy underside about 3.8cm (1$\frac{1}{2}$in) in from the edge and glue down securely to hold the horse in place.
Position the other three horses at regular intervals around the canopy.

## Assembly

Fit the roof onto the canopy underside and glue in place.

Cut off one of the ends of the metal reel. Fasten the reel to the centre of the base with strong glue. Put some glue around the edge of reel and place the cardboard tube over it (Fig.1). Hold tube firmly until it feels secure.

Push the dowel through the canopy underside and roof until about 2.5cm *(1in)* protrudes at the top. Glue felt decorations over the dowel to cover the edges of the hole. Cover the end of the dowel with felt and glue the wooden ball on the top.

Pass the dowel through the centre column and insert the end into the hole in the metal reel (Fig.2). The underside of the canopy will rest on the centre column. You can rotate the canopy and horses by turning the knob at the top.

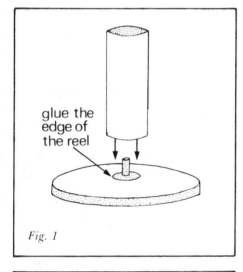

glue the edge of the reel

*Fig. 1*

*Fig. 2*

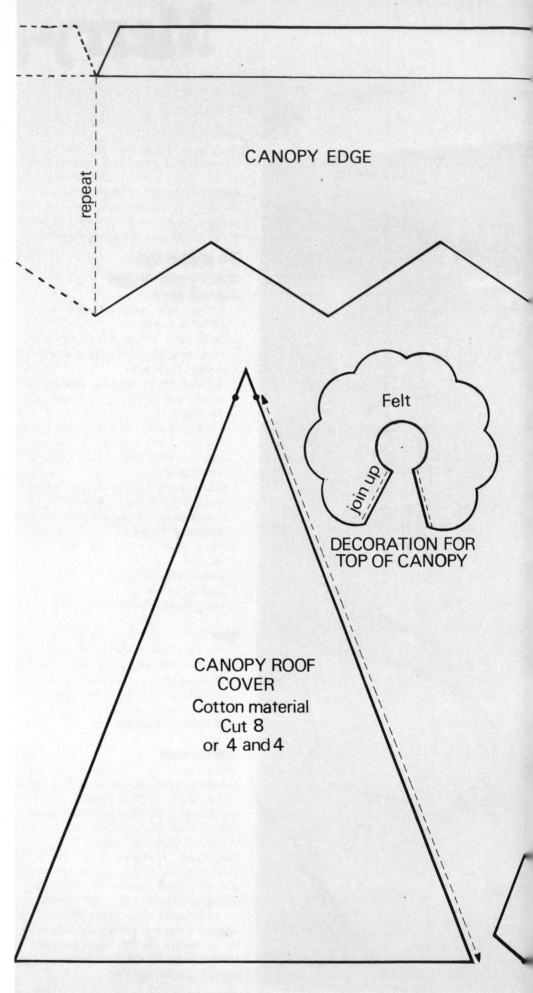

repeat

CANOPY EDGE

Felt

join up

DECORATION FOR TOP OF CANOPY

CANOPY ROOF COVER

Cotton material
Cut 8
or 4 and 4

# Trace patterns for merry-go-round

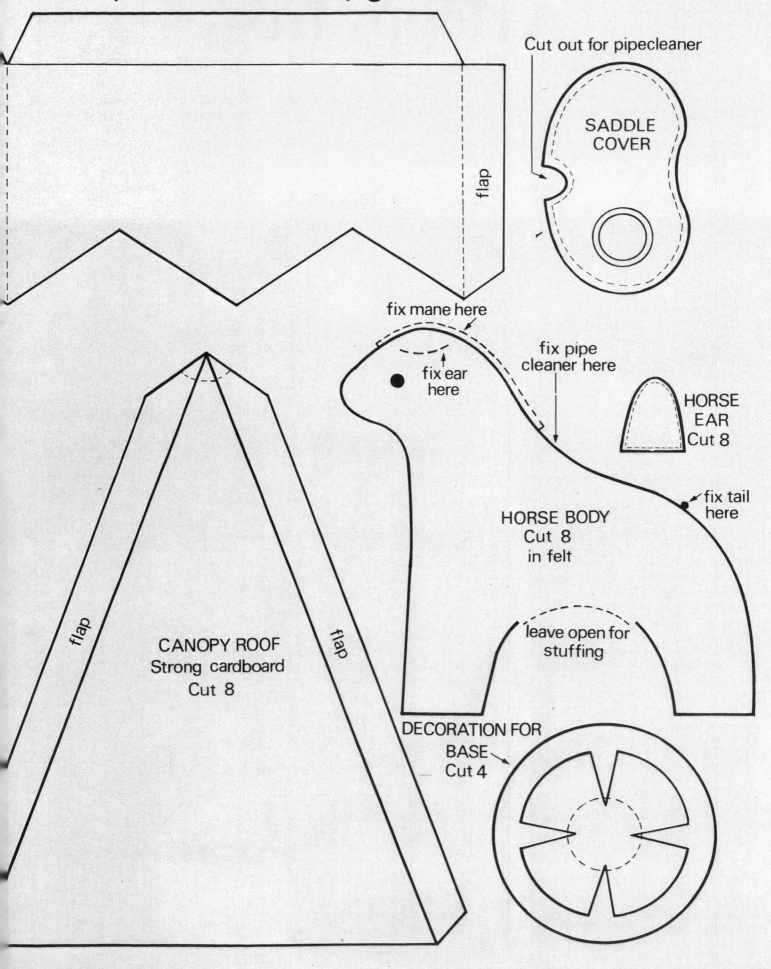

Cut out for pipecleaner

SADDLE COVER

flap

fix mane here

fix pipe cleaner here

fix ear here

HORSE EAR Cut 8

fix tail here

HORSE BODY Cut 8 in felt

flap

flap

CANOPY ROOF Strong cardboard Cut 8

leave open for stuffing

DECORATION FOR BASE Cut 4

# A floppy frog

This floppy frog is made from a simple pattern in soft green and beige suede and filled with beans or polystyrene beads. If you use the latter, or lentils, for the filling you will need to put weights in the frog's legs. The toy could also be made up in firm fabric instead of suede in the colour of your choice. Here is a popular gift for any occasion.

## To make the frog
### You will need:

☐ 2.5cm *(1in)* squared graph paper, for pattern
☐ sharp scissors
☐ 1 piece of beige suede, 35.5cm by 30.5cm *(14in by 12in)*
☐ 1 piece of emerald green suede, 35.5cm *(14in)* square
☐ clear adhesive [cellophane] tape to secure the pattern when cutting out
☐ matching thread
☐ medium heavy sewing machine needle, or glover's needle, if the frog is to be hand sewn
☐ two large, flat black buttons for the eyes
☐ 2½lb *(1.25kg)* dried beans or lentils, or 7 cups of expanded polystyrene beads for filling.

# Graph pattern for frog

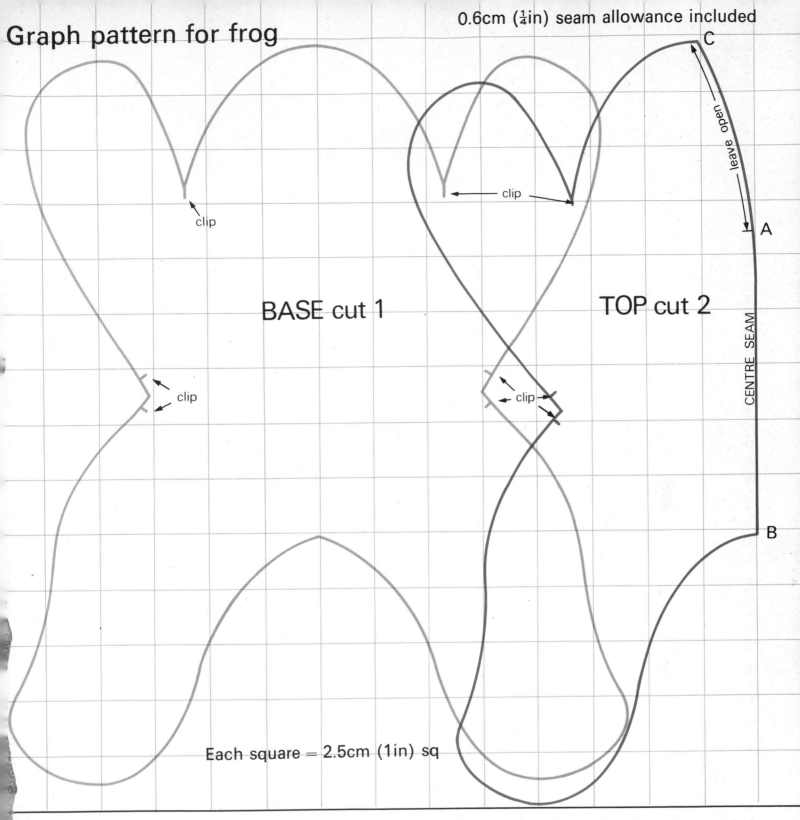

0.6cm (¼in) seam allowance included

C

leave open

A

CENTRE SEAM

B

clip

clip

clip

clip

BASE cut 1

TOP cut 2

Each square = 2.5cm (1in) sq

**To make the pattern**
Draw up a paper pattern of both pattern pieces from the graph, in which one square equals 2.5cm (1in). Seam allowances of 0.6cm (¼in) are given throughout.

**To cut out the front**
Using adhesive [cellophane] tape secure the two pattern pieces for the top to the nap side of the green suede. Make sure that the nap runs in the same direction on both pieces and cut the pieces out with a sharp pair of scissors. Cut one base piece from the beige suede in the same way.

**To join top sections**
Tack [baste] the two top sections together from A to B, leaving section A to C open for turning. Stitch along tacked [basted] length for strength. Clip round curved edges of joined section.

**Joining frog halves**
Place the joined green shape on top of the beige shape, wrong sides together, and tack [baste] together round the outside. Leave unstitched portion of green centre seam open. Stitch outside seam twice for strength, and clip seams.

**To finish**
Turn frog right side out and fill with beans (if you use lentils or polystyrene beads put weights in the frog's legs). Slip stitch the unstitched portion of the centre seam. Glue on black buttons for eyes, one each side of the frog's head, as shown.

# Teddy bears

This teddy bear can be made up in three sizes (large 66.5cm *(26¼in)* long; medium 56cm *(22in)* long; or small 42cm *(16½in)* long). The same basic pattern can be used to make a dog and rabbit.

**You will need:**

List (i)

☐ 140cm *(54in)* wide fur fabric
   0.70m *(¾ yd)* for large size
   0.50m *(½ yd)* for medium size
   0.35m *(⅜ yd)* for small size
☐ matching thread
☐ matching and black heavy carpet or button thread; carpet or fabric glue
☐ kapok or foam rubber chips
☐ a pair of eye buttons
☐ a small piece of black felt, for nose tip
☐ a small piece of dark pink felt for tongue

**For the soles and paws:**

☐ either a 23cm *(9in)* square of felt or a piece of leather cloth, bonded velvet or similar fabric:–
   11.5cm *(4½in)* by 46cm *(18in)* for large size
   11.5cm *(4½in)* by 33cm *(13in)* for medium size
   11.5cm *(4½in)* by 25.5cm *(10in)* for small size
☐ A small quantity of black knitting wool [yarn].

**For dressing the bears**

List (ii)   **Large size**
Waistcoat: 30.5cm *(12in)* by 61cm *(24in)* felt or similar fabric
Apron: 30.5cm *(12in)* by 79cm *(31in)* fabric and 1.90m *(75in)* of 1.3cm *(½in)* tape [seam binding]
Dress: 84cm *(33in)* by 30.5cm *(12in)* fabric and 1.40m *(57in)* narrow ribbon
   **Medium size**
Waistcoat: 23cm *(9in)* by 48.5cm *(19in)* felt or similar fabric

Apron: 23cm *(9in)* by 58.5cm *(23in)* fabric and 1.50m *(60in)* of 1.3cm *(½in)* tape [seam binding]
Dress: 73.5cm *(29in)* by 25.5cm *(10in)* fabric and 1.20m *(45in)* narrow ribbon
   **Small size**
Waistcoat: 38cm *(15in)* by 18cm *(7in)* felt or similar fabric
Apron: 18cm *(7in)* by 43cm *(17in)* fabric and 1.20m *(45in)* of 1.3cm *(½in)* tape [seam binding]
Dress: 56cm *(22in)* by 18cm *(7in)* fabric and 86.5cm *(34in)* narrow ribbon
☐ Lace for trimming apron and dress
☐ Matching threads

## To make the teddy bears

Using graph paper draw each pattern piece to scale from graph A. For the large size one square = 3cm *(1¼in)*

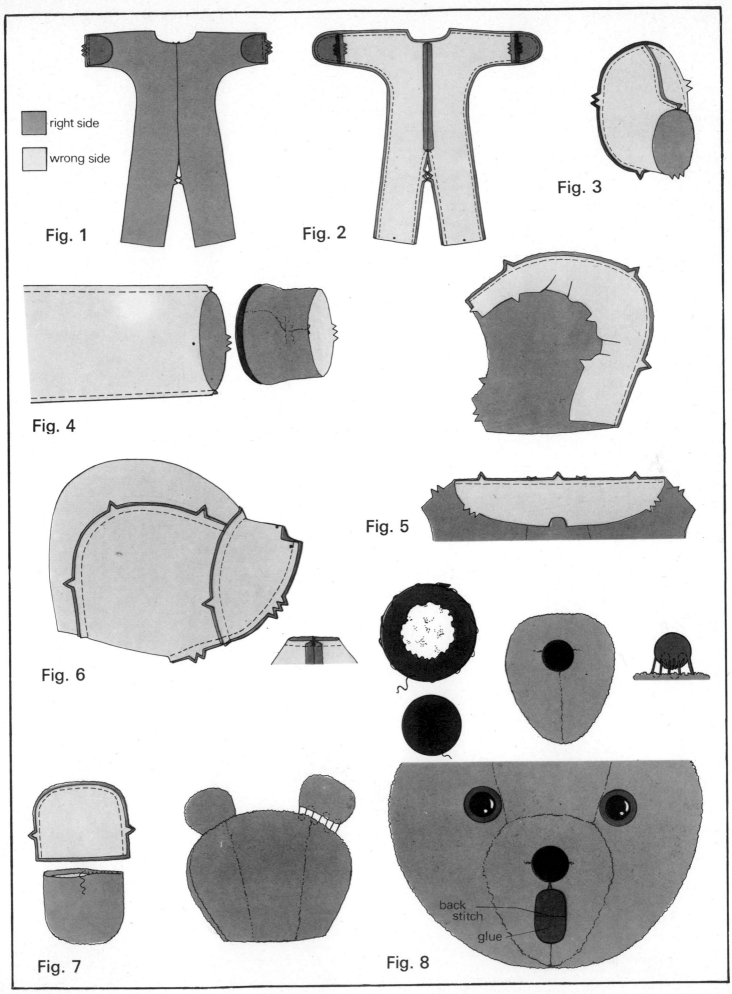

right side

wrong side

Fig. 1

Fig. 2

Fig. 3

Fig. 4

Fig. 5

Fig. 6

Fig. 7

Fig. 8

back stitch

glue

square, for the medium size it equals 2.5cm *(1in)* square and for the small size it equals 2cm *(¾in)* square. There is a seam allowance of 0.6cm *(¼in)*.

Cut out pattern pieces and mark all dots and notches and straight of grain line. Fold the fabric in half with selvedges together and place the centre head on the fold, the back, front, head and foot once and the ear twice on double fabric. Cut nose once on single fabric.

Take care that the grain line on the pattern lies on the straight grain of the fabric. Pin into place and cut out.

Cut one nose tip from black felt, one tongue from pink felt and two soles and two front paws from contrasting fabric. Transfer all markings from the pattern pieces to the fabric.

With right sides together and matching notches tack [baste] and stitch the centre-front and centre-back seams. With right sides together and matching notches tack and stitch the front paws to the front arms (Fig.1).

With right sides together and matching notches tack [baste] and stitch the back to the front on the inside leg seam, stretching the back to fit the front.

With right sides together and matching notches tack [baste] and stitch the front to the back from the neckline, down the arms, round the paws and underarm seams to the lower edges of the legs (Fig.2).

**The feet and head**

With right sides together, tack [baste] and stitch centre-front seam of feet. Clip curve. With right sides together and matching notches, and the centre-front seam of the foot to the sole, tack [baste] and stitch the foot to the sole (Fig.3). Turn to the right side.

Push the foot inside the leg of the body, and, with right sides together and matching notches and the centre-front seam of the foot to the dot on the leg, tack [baste] and stitch. Turn body to right side (Fig.4).

With right sides together and matching notches tack [baste] and stitch the side heads to the centre head.

With right sides together and matching notches tack [baste] and stitch the nose piece to the head (Fig.5).

With right sides together and matching notches and nose seam, tack [baste] and stitch from the dot, round the nose and under the jaw to the neckline.

Place the dot at the top of this seam to the dot at the centre-front of the nose. Tack [baste] and stitch across (Fig.6).

Turn the head to the right side and attach the eyes, either by sewing on with strong thread, if they have shanks, or by placing in position on the right

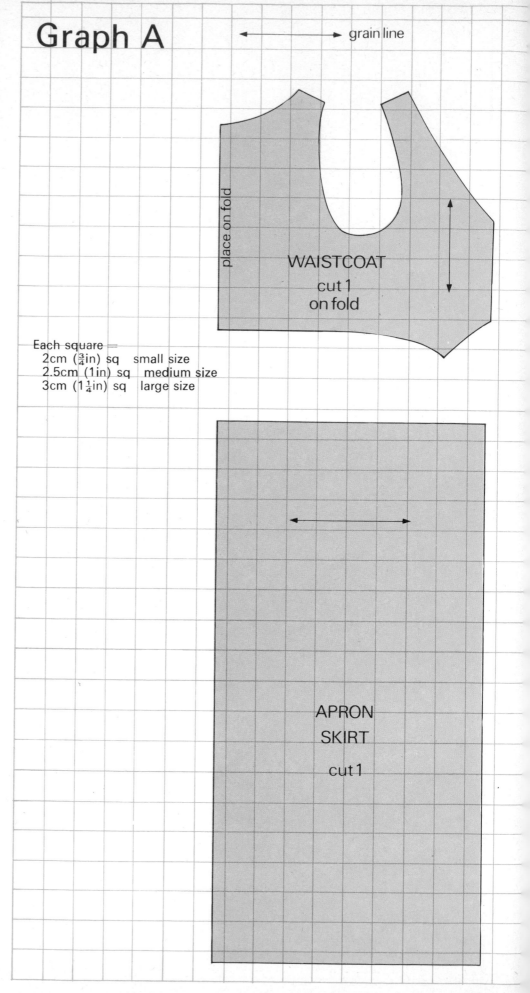

Graph A

grain line

place on fold

WAISTCOAT
cut 1
on fold

Each square =
2cm (¾in) sq   small size
2.5cm (1in) sq   medium size
3cm (1¼in) sq   large size

APRON

SKIRT

cut 1

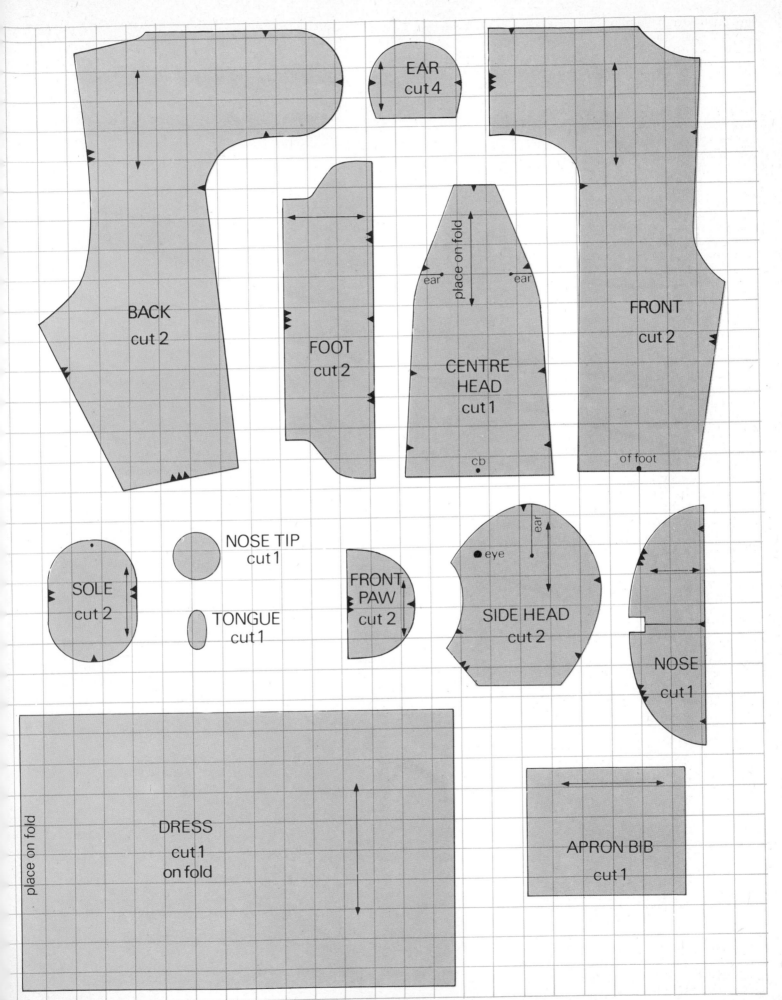

BACK
cut 2

EAR
cut 4

FOOT
cut 2

CENTRE
HEAD
cut 1

place on fold

ear

ear

cb

FRONT
cut 2

of foot

NOSE TIP
cut 1

SOLE
cut 2

TONGUE
cut 1

FRONT
PAW
cut 2

eye

ear

SIDE HEAD
cut 2

NOSE
cut 1

place on fold

DRESS

cut 1
on fold

APRON BIB

cut 1

side and pressing on the metal holder from the back.

Stuff the body and the head, pushing the stuffing well into the feet, paws and nose first.

### Finishing the head

With right sides together and matching notches, tack [baste] and stitch the outside curved edge of the ears. Turn to the right side. Turn in 0.6cm ($\frac{1}{4}$in) on lower edge and slip-stitch together.

Place the ear on the line indicated on the head and securely slip-stitch with strong matching thread (Fig.7).

**Nose.** Using strong black thread and leaving the end free, work large oversewing [overcasting] stitches over the edge. Place stuffing centrally and pull up the thread to form a ball.

Place one side of this to the centre-front of the nose so that it touches the small seam line.

Stitch the nose tip on to the nose by working a stitch through the fur fabric and then through the ball approximately half way from the stitching at the back. Fasten off securely.

Using black knitting wool [yarn] work two straight stitches 1.3cm ($\frac{1}{2}$in) to 2.5cm (1in) long to form a V on the seam line under the nose tip.

**Tongue.** Place the fold line centrally to the end of the straight black stitch. Back stitch on the fold line, fold the top tongue over and glue to the lower tongue with the glue (Fig.8).

### Attaching the head

Match the centre-fronts of the head and body, the centre-back of the head to the centre-back seam of the body and the shoulder seams of the body to the seams of the head. Join together with small stitches. Take the needle through the fabric 0.6cm ($\frac{1}{4}$in) from the edges first of the head and then the body. Pull up the thread every two or three stitches. For extra strength it is advisable to work at least two rows of stitching here. Fasten off securely.

To fluff up the pile brush the whole body gently, especially on the seam lines.

### Dressing the teddy bears

Using graph paper draw each pattern piece to scale and cut out. The scale is the same as for the body pieces.

**Waistcoat.** With right sides together join the shoulder seams, taking 0.6cm ($\frac{1}{4}$in) turnings [seam allowance].

From the right side work a row of straight or zig-zag machine stitching 0.6cm ($\frac{1}{4}$in) from the raw edges. Cut buttonholes on one front and attach buttons to correspond on the other.

**Apron.** Turn up the lower edge 3.2cm ($1\frac{1}{4}$in) and machine stitch into place. Turn to the right side and attach the lace over the stitching. On the wrong side make a small hem on the side edges of the bib and skirt.

Work a row of gathering stitches along the top end of the skirt and pull up to half the waist measurement. Cut a piece of tape [seam binding] twice the waist measurement and mark the centre, placing this on the right side of the apron on top of the gathers. Hold in place with a row of straight or zig-zag machine stitching on the tape. At the top of the bib turn under 3cm ($1\frac{1}{4}$in) and finish as for the lower edge. Cut the remaining tape [seam binding] in half lengthways. Place on the right side of the bib 0.6cm ($\frac{1}{4}$in) from each side and stitch with a straight or zig-zag machine stitch. Place centre front of lower edge of bib to centre of tape. Hold in place with a row of straight or zig-zag stitching. Fasten off all ends securely.

**Dress.** With right sides together join the centre-back seam, taking 0.6cm ($\frac{1}{4}$in) turnings [seam allowance].

Neaten the edges together by zig-zag machine stitch or oversewing [overcasting]. Turn up a small hem on to the wrong side and stitch on the edge. Attach lace on to the other raw edge.

Work rows of elastic shirring, starting 0.6cm ($\frac{1}{4}$in) from the lace and continuing to the required length.

Fasten off the ends securely on the wrong side. Cut the ribbon into three equal lengths.

Sew two lengths to top of dress, tie a bow with the rest and sew in place.

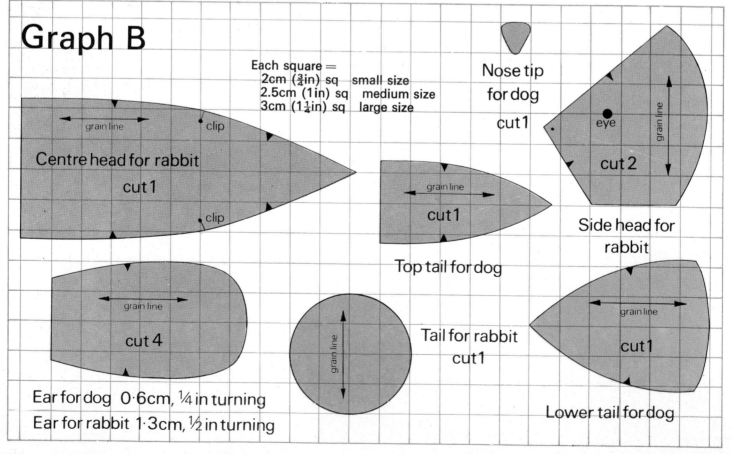

Graph B

Each square =
2cm ($\frac{3}{4}$in) sq   small size
2.5cm (1in) sq   medium size
3cm ($1\frac{1}{4}$in) sq   large size

Nose tip for dog
cut 1

grain line   clip
Centre head for rabbit
cut 1
clip

eye
cut 2
Side head for rabbit

grain line
cut 1

grain line
cut 4

grain line
Top tail for dog

grain line
Tail for rabbit
cut 1

grain line
cut 1

Ear for dog  0·6cm, ¼ in turning
Ear for rabbit 1·3cm, ½ in turning

Lower tail for dog

# Two cuddly companions

Here are two more soft toys that you can make as gifts that children will treasure. For each animal follow list (i) of materials for teddy bear on page 30, with the exception of the materials for soles and paws. The clothes also fit the dog and rabbit.

**Additional materials you will need**
For each toy:–
☐ 0.45m (½yd) of contrasting fabric
☐ thin cardboard for nose tip (for dog)
☐ 0.90m (1yd) of 2.5cm (1in) wide ribbon

## The Dog

Using graph paper draw the main body to the size required using the basic teddy bear graph pattern A.
Draw the head pieces to scale from the basic pattern A too, then draw two tail pieces and the ear piece from graph pattern B.
The body back, front, side head, two ear pieces and top tail should be cut from one fabric and the centre head, the soles, paws and the other two ear pieces from the contrasting fabric.
Make up the body and head in the same way as the bear.

### To finish the head
**Ears.** Slip stitch the ears to the head seams so that the front edge of the ear is 6.5cm (2½in) away from nose seam.
**Nose.** Using the pattern piece for the nose tip, cut a piece of cardboard. Cut a piece of felt approx. 0.3cm (⅛in) larger than the cardboard all around.
Work a row of gathering around the outside edge of the felt. Place the card centrally on the felt. Pull up the gathering thread so that the edge of the felt overlaps the card tightly. Slip stitch the nose tip onto the nose where indicated.
**Tongues and eyes.** These are made up in the same way as on the bear.
Tie ribbon around neck in a bow.

### Tail
With right sides together and matching notches, tack [baste] and stitch the top tail to the lower tail leaving the straight ends open. Turn through and stuff tail, turn in the ends and slip-stitch. Stitch the tail to the back of the dog at the base of the back body.

## The Rabbit

From graph pattern A draw the basic body to scale. From graph pattern B draw the head pieces, ear and tail to scale. Cut front paws, front ears, centre head and feet from contrasting fabric and rest of pieces from main fabric.
Make up the basic body in the same way as the teddy bear. Make up the basic head in the same way as the bear, but using the new head pieces from graph B that you have cut out.

### To finish the head
Make up the ears but do not stuff. After slip-stitching the raw edges together, fold the lower edge of the ear in half and slip-stitch to the head so that the inside edge of the ear is level with the seamline. The tongue, eyes and nose should be worked in the same way as for the teddy bear.
Tie ribbon around neck in a bow.

### Tail
Using strong matching thread and leaving the end free work large over-sewing [overcasting] stitches over the edge. Place the stuffing centrally and pull up the thread to form a ball. Stitch tail to the back of the rabbit.

# Snakes and ladders

Make this exciting game of Snakes and Ladders in felt. A game for 2–6 players, the object is to reach the last square first. A dice is thrown by the participants in turn and the number thrown indicates the number of squares a player must move his coloured counter. A six must be thrown before a player can move from the starting square. When a player lands on a square at the base of a ladder he must ascend it, and when he lands on a square with a snake's head he must descend it. To end the game a player must throw the exact number of remaining squares to land on 100.

## Materials you will need:

To make a cloth approximately 91cm (36in) square

☐ 0.9m (1yd) red felt 91cm (36in) wide
☐ two 30.5cm (12in) squares in both green and yellow felt
☐ glue suitable for fabric
☐ one 46cm (18in) square purple felt
☐ approximately 13.7m (15yds) fine white piping cord
☐ 2 skeins black soft embroidery cotton [six-strand embroidery thread]
☐ black sewing thread and white thread
☐ 2m (2¼yd) narrow braid (optional)
☐ gold beads or sequins for eyes and thick gold thread for tongues
☐ pair of No.5 [9] knitting needles; one No.1 [13] needle; chenille embroidery needle
☐ ball point pen or soft pencil

## To make the cloth

Cut thirty-two 5cm (2in) squares from the green felt and 32 from the yellow felt. Straighten the edges of the square of red felt and measure 20.5cm (8in) in from each side. Draw a 51cm (20in) square very lightly in the centre of the red felt, leaving a 20.5cm (8in) border all round.

Divide this central square into a hundred 5cm (2in) squares, marked lightly. Pin the yellow and green squares at random inside the drawn lines, leaving 36 squares uncovered, to create a pleasing three-coloured playing area.

Tack [baste] the squares in position and stitch in place along the edges, using an open zig-zag stitch and black thread. Take care not to close up the zig-zag too much as this causes the felt to buckle. Alternatively, hem each square in place by hand, or leave the tacking [basting] stitches in position until the squares have been embroidered, then remove them and stick the squares in place at the corners with glue.

On every fourth square lightly draw the relevant numeral, working across and back along the lines of squares in the order of play. Embroider the numbers in stem stitch, using soft embroidery thread and a chenille needle, making each as large as possible.

Sew narrow braid around the outside of the playing area if desired, either by hand or with a large machine stitch.

## Snakes and ladders

Draw the snakes on the purple felt, and cut out, following the curves as illustrated.

To make the smallest ladder, cast on 8 stitches, using the piping cord and No.5 [9] needles.

**1st row** K.
**2nd row** *K1, wind cord twice round needle, rep from * to last st, K1.
**3rd row** *K1, drop next two loops, rep from * to last st, K1.

Pull down row 2 so that the loops are even.

**4th row** using a No.1 [13] needle, cast off. Make six more ladders in the same way, casting on 10, 12, 14, 18, 20 and 24 stitches respectively.

Pin out the 'rungs' evenly in each ladder and press under a damp cloth.

## To complete the cloth

Arrange the snakes and ladders on the cloth, spacing them over the whole area and overlapping them occasionally to add greater interest to the game.

Make sure that each begins and ends on a square, allowing for tongues to be added to the head of each snake. Take care not to obscure the embroidered numbers.

Either hem the snakes in place neatly by hand, or glue them down. Attach gold beads or sequins to the head for eyes, and work a circle of stem stitch around each bead in black thread.

Work the tongues by stitching a piece of thick gold thread to the head of each snake, or alternatively, embroider a tongue in chain stitch, using thick gold stranded cotton [thread]. Hem ladders in place lightly with white thread.

# Doll nightie case

Make bedtime a happy time for a little girl with this charming nightie case, made up exactly like a doll. Simple to make, this charming design would make an ideal present for any occasion.

**You will need:**

☐ 0.9m *(1yd)* patterned cotton fabric
☐ 0.9m *(1yd)* lining fabric in a toning or contrasting colour
☐ kapok or foam rubber chips
☐ small amount of wool [yarn] for hair
☐ sewing thread to match fabrics
☐ embroidery thread
☐ felt scraps for eyes and mouth

## To make the nightie case

Draw up the pattern pieces from the graph given.

Cut all the pieces for the head, hands and legs from the lining fabric, together with the lining for the dress. From main fabric, cut dress, arms and mob cap.

There is no seam allowance included on the graph, so add 1.3cm *(½in)* to all edges when cutting out.

With right sides facing, machine stitch the hands and legs together in pairs, and stitch the two head pieces together, leaving all the straight edges open.

Turn to the right side and press all the pieces. Stuff the hands, legs and head with kapok, and oversew [overcast] the raw edges to close.

With right sides facing, fold the arms in half widthways and machine stitch along the side seams.

Fold back 3.8cm *(1½in)* at the cuff end and press on the line marked 'cuff edge'. Run a gathering thread along the line indicated on the pattern piece. Turn the arms right side out and insert a hand into each cuff opening, thumbs pointing downwards. Pin into position, as shown (Fig.1).

Pull up the gathers and machine stitch along the gathering line indicated on

Fig. 1

front r.s.

Fig. 2

top neck edge

lining

Fig. 3

Fig. 4

Fig. 5

Fig. 6

pattern to secure the hands in place.
Pin and tack [baste] the arms and legs in place on the right side of the dress front, as shown (Fig.2).

**Dress.** With the right sides facing, place the two dress backs on the dress front, matching side seams, and stitch together at the sides, securing the arms in position. Machine stitch the side seams of the dress lining and press open. With right sides facing, pin and tack [baste] the lining to the top of the dress and machine stitch together. (The lining will not reach the bottom edge of the dress.)

With wrong sides facing, make a fold along the line marked 'neck edge' on the dress, 3.8cm *(1½in)* from the top edge, and press. (The lining should now reach to the bottom of the dress).

Run a gathering thread along the seam line attaching the lining to the dress (Fig.3).

With right sides facing, pin and tack [baste] the back seams of the dress and the dress lining, from the bottom edge to (*) (Fig.4). Press both seams open. With right sides facing, pin and tack [baste] bottom edges of the dress together and stitch, securing the legs in position between the two layers of fabric. With right sides facing, machine stitch the bottom edges of the lining together. Turn the lining right side out, over the dress 'bag', and turn in the seam allowances on the back openings from (*) to the neck edge (Fig.5).

Hem the lining neatly to the dress by hand.

Turn the dress right side out, insert the head in the neck opening and pin in position.

Pull up the gathers to form a frill around the neck, making sure that the back edges are together. Machine stitch along the line of gathers to secure the head to the dress.

Either embroider the eyes and the mouth on the head, or cut out from felt and sew in position as shown (Fig.6).

**Mob cap.** To make the cap, turn in and machine stitch a 0.6cm *(¼in)* hem all round the edge.

Run a gathering thread 2.5cm *(1in)* from the hemmed edge, pull up the gathers to fit and arrange the cap on the doll's head. Stitch firmly in place along the line of gathers, to secure the cap to the head.

**Hair.** Cut long strands of yarn, knot them at one end, and form the hair by taking small stitches all round the back and sides of the head, leaving long loops hanging between each stitch (Fig.6).

Make sure that the stitches are hidden beneath the frill of the cap.

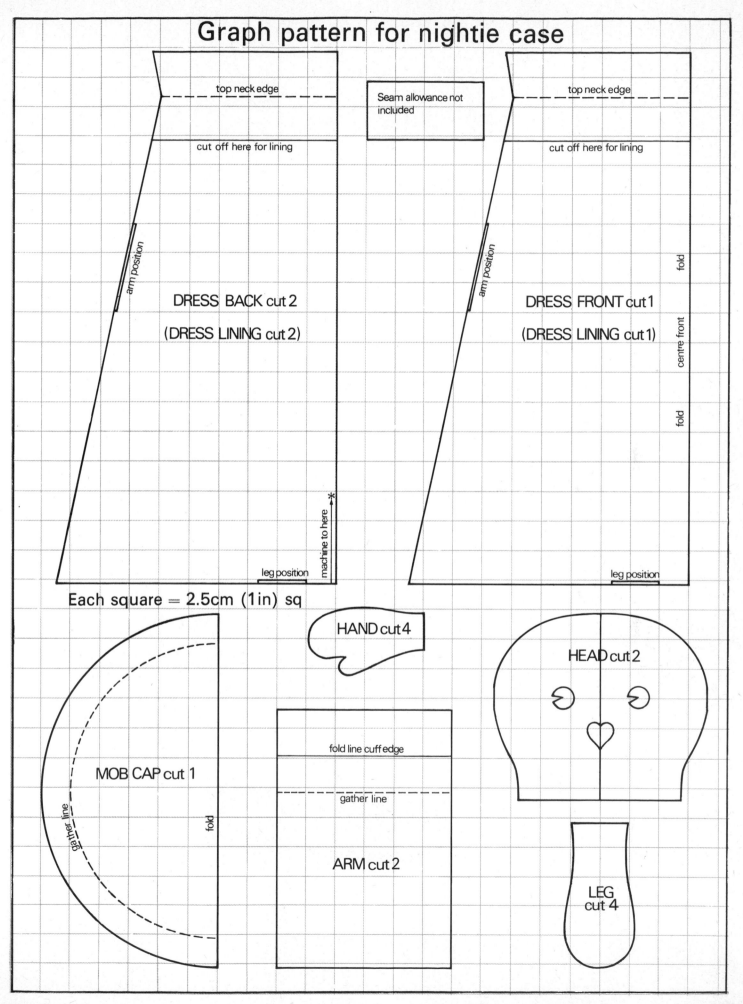

# Graph pattern for nightie case

top neck edge

Seam allowance not included

cut off here for lining

cut off here for lining

top neck edge

arm position

arm position

DRESS BACK cut 2

(DRESS LINING cut 2)

DRESS FRONT cut 1

(DRESS LINING cut 1)

fold

centre front

fold

machine to here

leg position

leg position

Each square = 2.5cm (1in) sq

HAND cut 4

HEAD cut 2

MOB CAP cut 1

gather line

fold

fold line cuff edge

gather line

ARM cut 2

LEG
cut 4

# Jack-in-the-box

This colourful clown Jack-in-the-box will delight and fascinate young children. Both the box and the clown are made from odd pieces of fabric and household materials and are not difficult to assemble.

**You will need:**

**Clown**

☐ small pieces of plain or patterned fabric

☐ matching thread

☐ 3 hair rollers 3cm ($1\frac{1}{4}in$) in diameter and 7.5cm (3in) long

☐ scraps of felt, double knitting wool [yarn], lace and embroidery silks

☐ linen thread

☐ kapok or foam rubber chips

☐ 2 small beads for eyes

**Box**

☐ strong cardboard

☐ 0.45m ($\frac{1}{2}yd$) cotton fabric to cover box

☐ 0.2m ($\frac{1}{4}yd$) PVC [fabric vinyl] to line box

☐ felt to line lid and base

☐ jewellery box lid fastening or button and loop

☐ glue suitable for fabric

## To make the clown

### Head

Trace off and cut out the pattern pieces given overleaf.

Cut the four head pieces from plain fabric and tack [baste] together, matching double and single notches. With right sides facing, stitch the pieces together using a small machine stitch and taking a 0.6cm ($\frac{1}{4}in$) seam allowance, which is allowed throughout on all seams.

Leave the neck opening free for turning and stuffing. Stuff the head very firmly with kapok, and oversew [overcast] the end to prevent the stuffing escaping.

Cut out the eye sockets and the mouth from bits of white felt and sew neatly in place on the clown's head.

Cut the nose and the clown's smile from pieces of red felt and sew it on top of the mouth.

Gather up the nose shape and stuff with a little kapok. Pull up the gathering thread and sew in position on the clown's face.

Sew two small beads to two small circles of the felt and attach them to the eye sockets.

To complete the features, embroider eyebrows and eyelashes in black embroidery thread and outline the mouth. To form the hair, cut enough lengths of double knitting wool [yarn], 7.5cm (3in) in length, to lay across the clown's head from front to back so that it extends down the sides of the head.

Work back stitch across the top of the head horizontally to secure the hair in place.

### Body

Sew the three hair rollers together end to end with linen thread.

Sew the head to the top hair roller, inserting the neck down inside the roller. Cut two main body pieces from either plain or patterned fabric. If using a plain fabric, cut shapes from felt to match the fabric on the box and sew them to the front of the clown.

Cut the four hand shapes from plain fabric and with right sides together, join each hand shape to the main body pieces, matching Bs and Cs.

With right sides together, place the two halves of the body together. Tack [baste] and stitch from the neck edge A, around the hands and down the side seams, leaving the neck and bottom edges open.

Turn to the right side and lightly stuff the hands with kapok.

Stab stitch the stuffing in place to form the fingers and thumbs, following the lines indicated on the trace pattern.

Slip the body of the clown over the rollers and sew the neck to the base of the head.

Sew a length of lace around the neck and catch the thumbs to the sides of the head.

## To make the box

Cut four side pieces from strong cardboard each 13cm (5in) by 11cm ($4\frac{1}{2}in$).

Cut one base piece 11cm ($4\frac{1}{2}in$) square and one piece 11.5cm ($4\frac{1}{2}in$) square, plus 1.3cm ($\frac{1}{2}in$) on three sides, to form the lid (Fig.1).

Cut pieces of fabric the size of all the box pieces, plus 1.3cm ($\frac{1}{2}in$) all round.

Cut the corners of the fabric to fit (Fig.2) and cover each cardboard piece. Secure in place by sticking a layer of PVC [fabric vinyl] on the inside of the pieces, cut slightly smaller than the cardboard itself.

Join the four side pieces together along the 13cm (5in) edges with strong thread, sewing on the wrong side wherever possible.

Join the sides of the lid section together and line the lid with a square of felt, stuck in position.

Sew the side of the lid without the flap to one side of the box. Attach the fastening to the opposite side of the lid and to the corresponding position on the front of the box.

Line the base of the box with felt.

Attach the bottom roller to a circular piece of cardboard 7.5cm (3in) in diameter, with glue and thread, and glue this to the base of the box.

Catch the main fabric of the clown to the felt lining of the base so that it covers the cardboard stand.

Insert base into box. Sew in place.

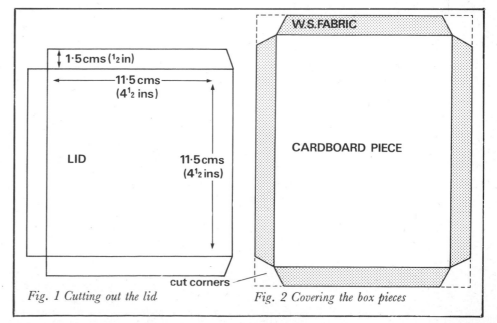

*Fig. 1 Cutting out the lid*     *Fig. 2 Covering the box pieces*

41

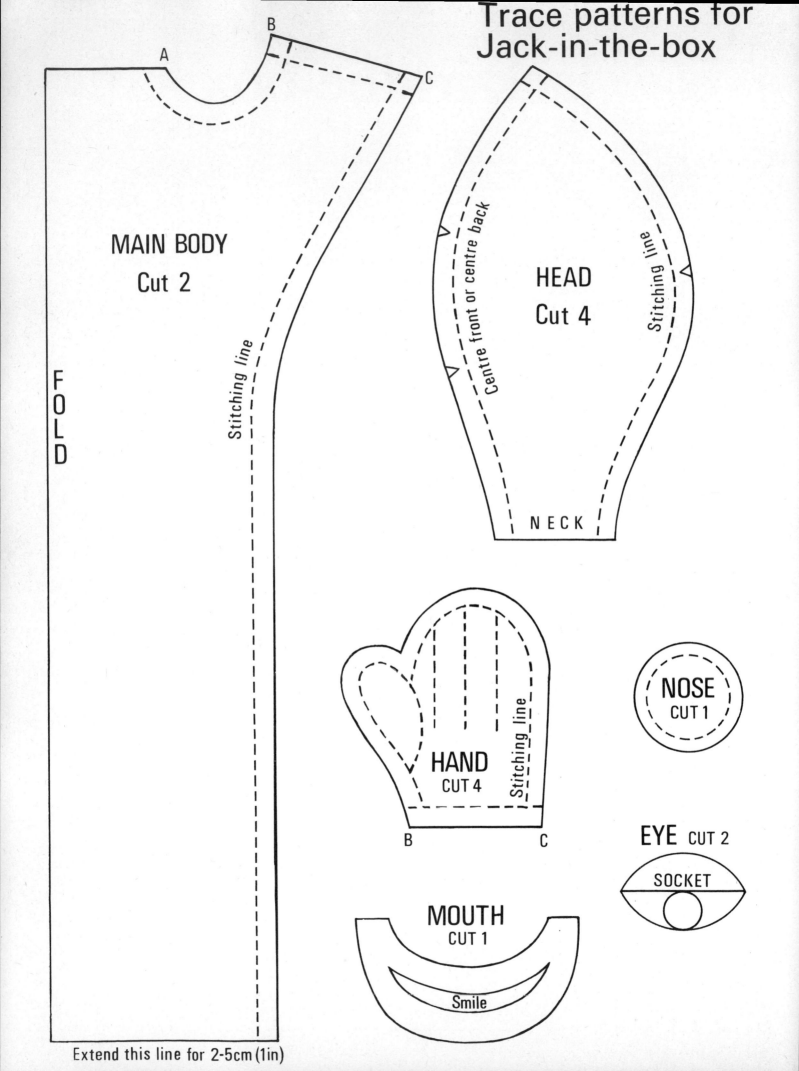

Trace patterns for
Jack-in-the-box

MAIN BODY
Cut 2

A B C

FOLD

Stitching line

Extend this line for 2-5cm (1in)

HEAD
Cut 4

Centre front or centre back

Stitching line

NECK

HAND
Cut 4

Stitching line

B C

NOSE
CUT 1

EYE CUT 2

SOCKET

MOUTH
CUT 1

Smile

# Bell nose

This enchanting toy is tremendously popular with young children. He is simple to make, using odd pieces of colourful fabrics, and as he bounces along on his elastic the reason for his name becomes clear.

**Materials you will need:**
☐ scraps of fabric
☐ kapok or foam rubber chips
☐ small bell
☐ 20cm *(8in)* strip of narrow elastic
☐ 2 sequins or buttons for eyes
☐ ball of double knitting wool [yarn] for hair

**Note:** 0.6cm *(¼in)* seam allowance is given throughout.

## To make Bell nose

Draw up the pattern pieces from the graph given.

Cut two head shapes A, from either felt or plain fabric.

If using felt, tack [baste] and oversew [overcast] the shapes together with wrong sides facing, leaving the straight edges open. For other fabrics, tack [baste] and stitch together with right sides facing, leaving the straight edges open, and then turn to the right side.

Stuff the head firmly with kapok and oversew [overcast] the neck edges together firmly by hand.

Cut two body pieces B, from odd pieces of patterned fabric. With right sides facing, tack [baste] and stitch the two halves together, leaving the neck, wrist and waist edges open.

Turn to the right side and fold over a small hem on the neck edge. Insert the head into the opening and neatly sew the neck firmly to the head, all the way round.

Cut four hand shapes C, from either felt or plain fabric.

If using felt, tack [baste] and oversew

[overcast] each pair of shapes together with wrong sides facing, leaving the straight edges open. For other fabrics, tack [baste] and stitch the pieces together with right sides facing leaving the straight edges open, and turn to the right side.

Stuff each hand firmly with kapok and oversew [overcast] the wrist edges together by hand.

Fold over a small hem on the wrist edges of the body piece B, and insert a hand into each opening. Sew the hands securely to the sleeves, all the way round.

Cut two trouser shapes D, from a contrasting fabric. With right sides facing, tack [baste] and stitch the two halves together, leaving the waist and ankle edges open.

Turn to the right side and fold over a small hem at the waist edge. Slip the body just inside the trousers and sew together all round, taking small pleats in the trousers where necessary to ensure a good fit.

Cut four boot shapes E, from either felt or plain fabric.

If using felt, tack [baste] and oversew [overcast] the shapes together with wrong sides facing, leaving the straight edges open.

For other fabrics, tack [baste] and stitch together with right sides facing, leaving the straight edges open, and turn to the right side.

Stuff each boot firmly with kapok and oversew [overcast] the ankle edges together firmly by hand.

Fold over a small hem on the lower edge of both trouser legs and insert a boot into each opening. Sew the trousers to the boots firmly all round.

**To complete the head**

To form the hair, wind the double knitting wool [yarn] around the four fingers of one hand, approximately twenty times. Break off the yarn and sew the loop of wool to the side of the head, half way down at ear level.

Continue to form loops in the same way, and sew them all round the back and sides of the head.

Cut two circular eyes from felt, and sew them neatly in position on the face. Sew sequins or buttons in the centres of the eyes to form the pupils.

Attach the bell to the centre of the face to form the nose.

Cut a smiling mouth shape from felt, and sew neatly in position under the bell.

If desired, cut several felt stars and sew them to the face and body. To complete, join the length of elastic to form a circle and sew the loop to the top of the head.

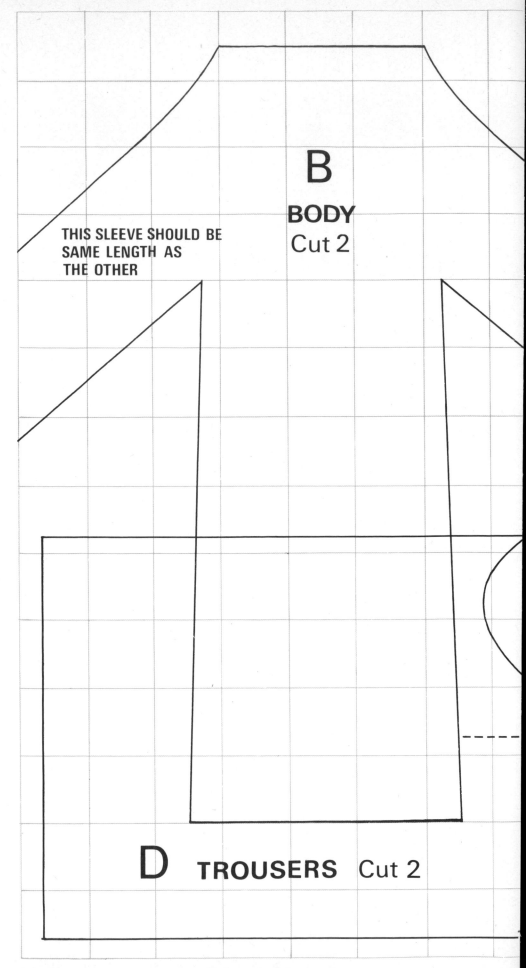

THIS SLEEVE SHOULD BE SAME LENGTH AS THE OTHER

**B**
**BODY**
Cut 2

**D** TROUSERS Cut 2

Each square equals 1·9cm (¾in) sq

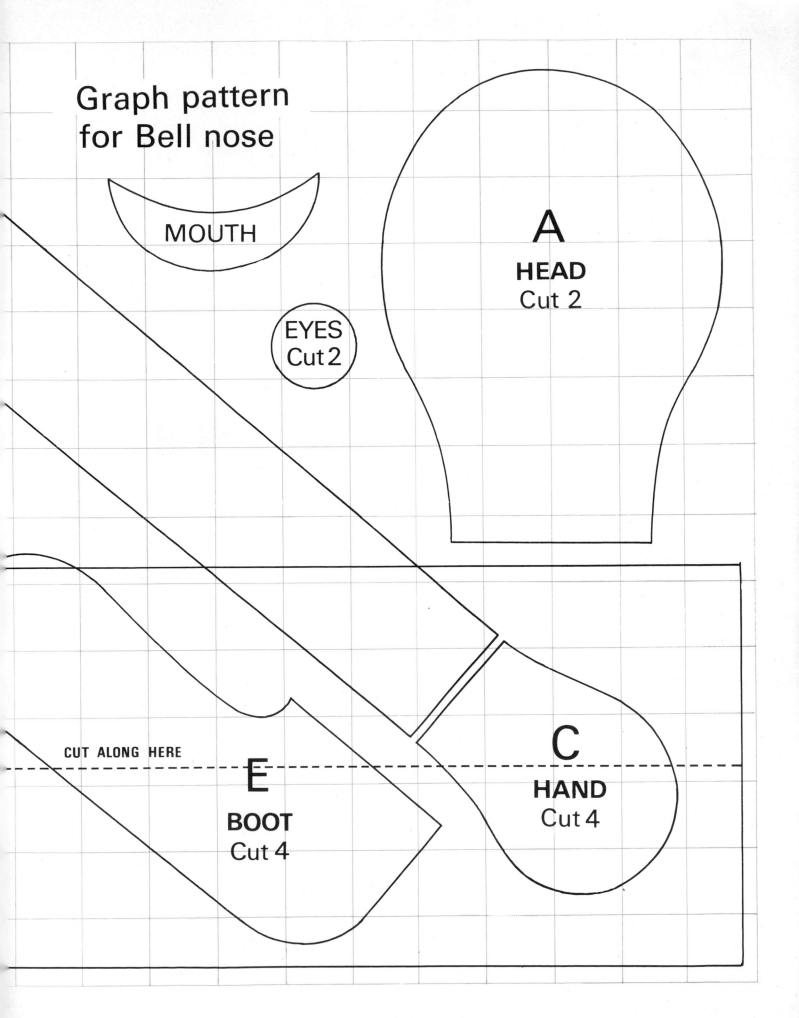

Graph pattern
for Bell nose

MOUTH

EYES
Cut 2

A
HEAD
Cut 2

CUT ALONG HERE

E
BOOT
Cut 4

C
HAND
Cut 4

# Punch and Judy

The bodies of these traditional puppets are attached to a cardboard base and the heads supported by sticks which are manipulated to make the puppets move.

**Materials you will need:**
**Punch and Judy**
☐ 0.3m *(⅓yd)* cotton fabric for each puppet, patterned or plain
☐ 0.2m *(¼yd)* pink fabric for hands and faces
☐ 2 dowel rods or sticks, 46cm *(18in)* long and about 1.3cm *(½in)* across
☐ glue suitable for fabric
☐ small amounts of felt, embroidery thread, lace, braid, beads, ribbon and double knitting yarn for decoration; kapok or foam rubber chips
☐ matching sewing thread
☐ cardboard tube approx. 25cm *(10in)* long and 9cm *(3½in)* in diameter, or sheet of cardboard approx. 25cm *(10in)* square for base
☐ clear adhesive [cellophane] tape
**Baby**
☐ 3 pipe cleaners
☐ piece of white fabric, 23cm *(9in)* by 14cm *(5½in)*
☐ small amounts of lace, pink felt, ribbon and kapok or foam chips
☐ matching thread
☐ packet of 1.3cm *(½in)* wide gauze bandage for binding the body

## To make Punch and Judy

Draw up all the pattern pieces onto squared paper, following the graph.
A 0.6cm *(¼in)* seam allowance has been included on all pattern pieces, except those cut from felt. The seam lines are marked by a dotted line on the pattern. Cut out the body pieces, two for each puppet, from the contrasting fabrics. For two puppets, cut eight hands and four head pieces from the pink fabric. With right sides facing, join the head pieces together in pairs, using a small machine stitch.
Clip seams. Turn to the right side.
Stuff firmly with kapok, paying special attention to the nose and chin.
Insert a wooden dowel or stick into each head for about 5cm *(2in)*, and carefully pack more stuffing around the rod.
Secure each head firmly to the rod by binding around the lower edges with cotton or linen thread.
With right sides facing, stitch the hand pieces to the body pieces, matching As and Bs.

If you wish to decorate the main part of the puppets by applying felt shapes and beads, do so at this stage before making up the bodies.
With right sides facing, stitch the body pieces together in pairs, sewing up the side seams, around the hands and up to the neck in a continuous seam. Leave the neck and bottom edges open.
Slip each body over the bottom of the rod and sew firmly to the neck edge by applying a gathered felt or lace collar.

### Punch
Cut out the hat from felt and decorate at this stage if desired. The Punch illustrated has zig-zag pieces of felt stitched to the top and lower edges of the hat, and felt shapes and coloured beads sewn onto the sides.
Oversew [overcast] the curved edges of the hat together, leaving the straight edges open.
Stuff firmly with kapok.
Cut lengths of double knitting wool [yarn] about 5cm *(2in)* long, and sew all round the back and sides of the head, just above the hat line, to form the hair. Sew the hat in position on the line indicated, so that the hair roots are enclosed.
Cut a felt mouth, and sew in position under the nose, as shown on the graph.
Cut two eyes from white felt, and sew in position. Cut two smaller circles of dark felt to form the pupils.

### Judy
To form the hair, cut length of double knitting wool [yarn] for about 46cm *(18in)* long. Sew the centre of the wool across the top of the head, form a centre parting and make a bun at the back by coiling the wool around. Sew the hair securely in place at the sides and back of the head.
Cut the crown and the brim for the hat from felt. Gather the crown where indicated on the pattern, and stitch to the brim as shown.
Place on the head, and catch at front and back to secure.
Form eyes and mouth as for Punch.
Cut the apron and the ties from either felt or fabric. If using fabric, turn under a small hem on all sides to neaten.
Attach a tie to each side of the apron, and tie and sew securely in place on the dress. The baby can be sewn onto apron.

### To complete the puppets
Cut two pieces of cardboard tubing,

approximately 12.5cm *(5in)* long and 9cm *(3½in)* in diameter.
Alternatively, use flat cardboard, and bend it when wet, letting it dry to shape around a bottle. Stick securely with clear adhesive [cellophane] tape to form the tubes. Cover each tube with felt and glue in place.
Decorate with beads and felt shapes, which can be either sewn or glued in place.
Attach the body of each puppet to the top of the tubes, so that they overlap by 1.3cm *(½in)*. Sew in place securely with linen thread.
To complete, attach braid around the top and bottom edges of the tubes.

## To make the baby

Make a frame using the three pipe cleaners. Take two pipe cleaners and twist them round each other at the centres. Bend two ends upwards and twist together to form the head and body.
Bend the other two ends downwards to form the legs.
Twist the third pipe cleaner round the body to form the arms, bending the ends back and twisting together to the correct length.
Bind the pipe cleaner figure with bandage, packing lightly in parts with kapok to give a reasonable body shape, paying special attention to the head and arms. Fasten with thread neatly to hold in place.
Cover the head, arms and legs with pieces of pink felt, oversewn [overcast] in place on the right side with matching thread. Sew some short lengths of yellow wool [yarn] to the head to form the hair, and embroider the features on the face.
Make a tiny bonnet from a piece of lace and sew in place on the head.
**Dress.** Take the piece of white fabric, stitch the two short ends together and turn to the right side. This forms the centre back seam of the baby's dress.
Turn up a hem at one end and sew a piece of lace to the edge of the fabric. Gather the other end of the dress to fit around baby's neck, and add a small lace frill.
Cut a small slit at each side of the dress for the armholes, and finish off neatly with a small turning [hem].
To complete, either gather the dress at the waist, or add a piece of ribbon to form a sash.

# Graph pattern for Punch and Judy

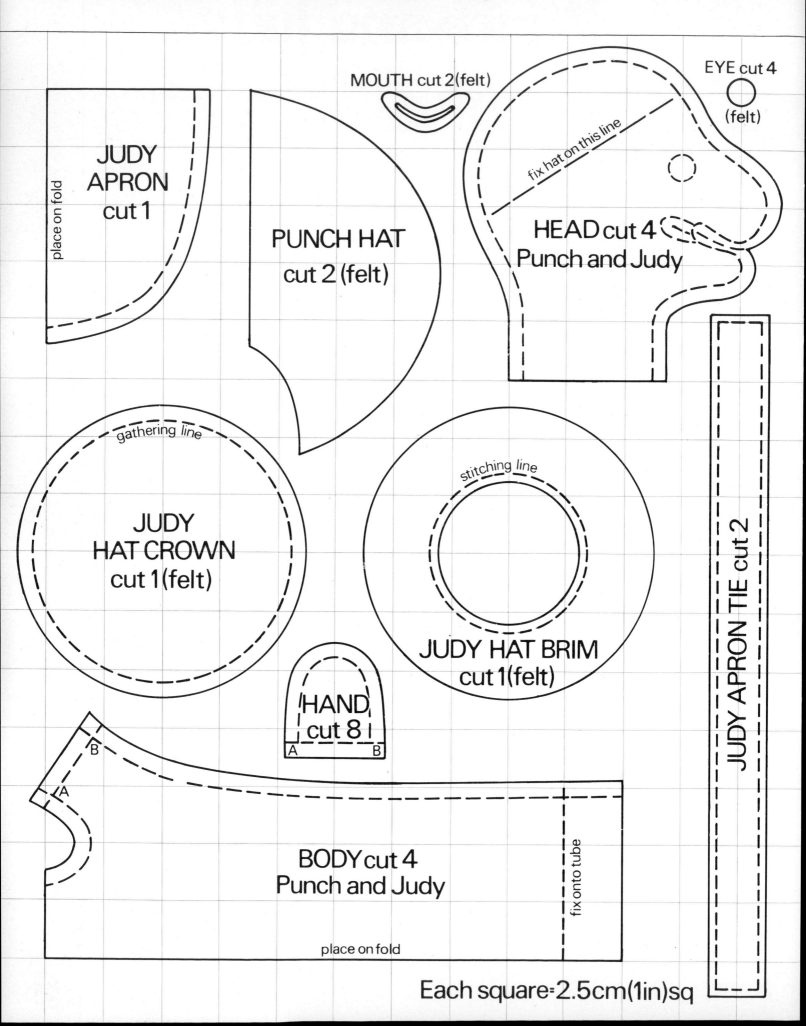

JUDY APRON cut 1

place on fold

MOUTH cut 2(felt)

PUNCH HAT cut 2 (felt)

HEAD cut 4 Punch and Judy

fix hat on this line

EYE cut 4 (felt)

gathering *line*

JUDY HAT CROWN cut 1(felt)

stitching *line*

JUDY HAT BRIM cut 1(felt)

JUDY APRON TIE cut 2

HAND cut 8

A B

B

A

BODY cut 4 Punch and Judy

fix onto tube

place on fold

Each square=2.5cm(1in)sq

# A hand puppet

Young children love to have their own soft toy or blanket to hug, so make up this simple yet lovable puppet as an unusual present.

## Materials you will need:

- ☐ 0.45m (½yd) fur fabric
- ☐ 0.45m (½yd) lining fabric in a contrasting colour
- ☐ small amount of stuffing for head
- ☐ scraps of felt or leather for eyes, mouth and collar
- ☐ thread to match fur fabric, lining fabric and eyes

## To make the puppet

Draw up the pattern pieces from the graph given onto squared paper.

A seam allowance of 0·6cm (¼in) is included on all edges on the graph.

Following the pattern layout given, cut the two body pieces, the ears, the head gusset and the head pieces from the fur fabric.

Make tailors' tacks to mark the positions of eyes, mouth and ears, as indicated on the pattern pieces.

Cut the body pieces, the head pieces and the head lining from the lining fabric.

The eyes and the mouth are cut from the contrast felt fabric or leather. For the mouth, cut a curved piece about 2·5cm (1in) by 0·5cm (¼in), and cut two circles of 1·3cm (½in) diameter for the eyes.

**Lining.** Pin, tack [baste] and stitch body piece 1 to body piece 2, at both side seams, stitching round the arms. Trim the corners and seams.

Fold the head lining piece in half as indicated on the pattern, and stitch the side edges and top curved edges together.

With right sides facing, stitch the head lining to the body lining, all around the neck edge, placing the seam on the head lining to the centre front of body piece 2.

**Body.** With right sides facing, pin, tack [baste] and stitch body pieces 1 and 2 together, as for lining. Clip the corners and trim the seams.

**Head.** Sew the eyes in position on each head piece, as indicated on the pattern. Sew the mouth in position on the head gusset, as indicated.

With right sides facing, pin, tack [baste] and stitch each ear lining to an ear piece, leaving an opening between X and X as indicated. Turn both ears to the right side and press.

With the fur fabric side uppermost, pin and tack [baste] each ear to a head piece, matching X and X as indicated.

With right sides facing tack [baste] and stitch the head gusset to each head piece. Begin at the front end by positioning the mouth correctly, and stitch in each direction separately, taking care not to distort the mouth.

Stuff the head firmly with kapok, or similar stuffing, leaving just enough space in the centre to insert a finger, so that the toy can also be used as a puppet.

### Joining body to lining

With right sides facing and matching seams, pin, tack [baste] and stitch the lining to the body around the circular outside edge.

Turn to the right side and press the stitched edge.

Attach the head to the body neatly by hand, centring the head between the arms. Turn in the raw edges to the wrong side, and sew the head to the fur fabric body only, leaving the lining free. Push the head lining up inside the head, and catch the lining neatly to the body around the neck edge, to secure in place and to prevent the stuffing from escaping.

To complete, cut a small length of ribbon or felt·and attach it around the outside of the neck to form a collar.

**Note:** The fur fabric pile can be eased out of the seams with a pin, so that all seams are as unnoticeable as possible.

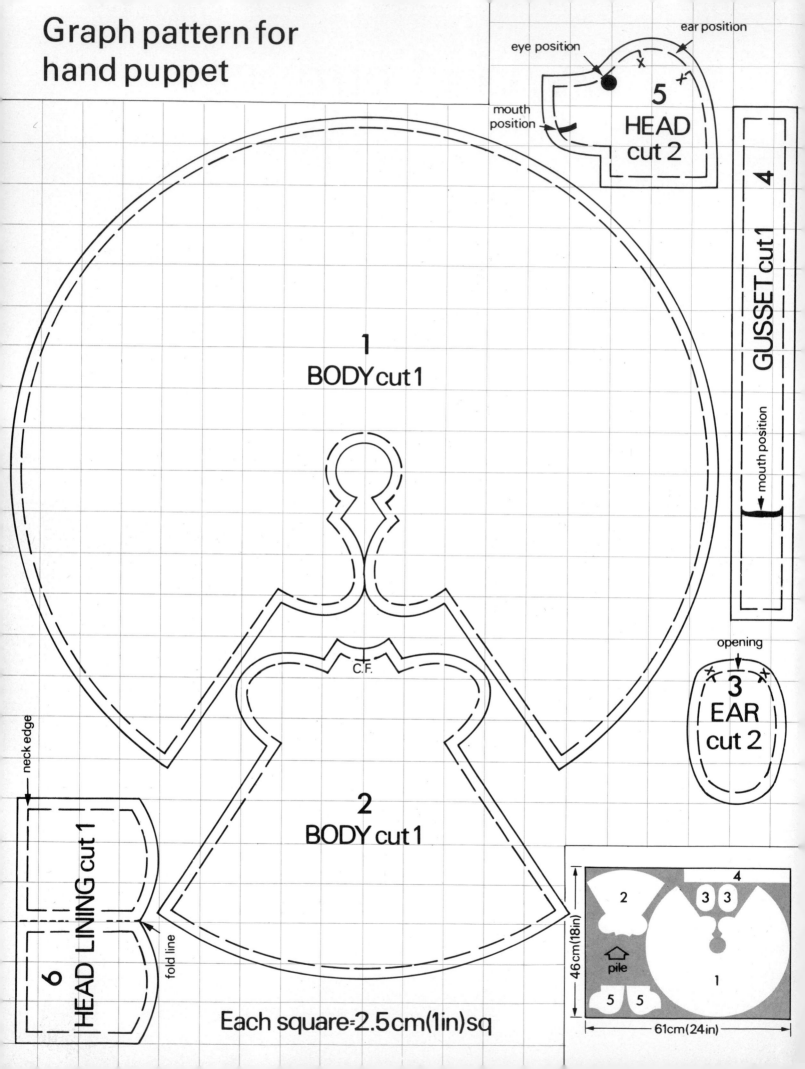

Graph pattern for hand puppet

5
HEAD
cut 2

eye position

ear position

mouth position

GUSSET cut 1

4

mouth position

1
BODY cut 1

C.F.

opening

3
EAR
cut 2

neck edge

2
BODY cut 1

fold line

6
HEAD LINING cut 1

Each square = 2.5 cm (1 in) sq

4

2

3  3

pile

5  5

1

46 cm (18 in)

61 cm (24 in)

# Finger puppets

Children will amuse themselves for hours playing with finger puppets. They are easy to put together and the four shown here, Eskimo, Hula girl, Arab and Geisha girl, could be made in just an evening. Experiment with lots of different nationalities and build up a collection.

## Materials you will need for four puppets:

- ☐ 30.5cm *(12in)* square felt in each colour, white, brown, purple and turquoise
- ☐ 10cm *(4in)* square felt in beige, cream, black and green
- ☐ scraps of felt in a variety of colours
- ☐ white, brown, purple and turquoise thread
- ☐ glue suitable for fabric

## To make the puppets

### 1. Eskimo

Trace off the pattern for the Eskimo. Cut out body front, top back body, lower back body and waistband in white felt, the hands and face in beige felt, the leg insets in cream felt and the fish and features in any scraps that you have available.

Snip around the front body head and waistband to make points for fur. Stick the boot insets to the body and work three cross stitches over them in brown thread. Work three more cross stitches at the neck (see Fig.1).

Glue the waistband to the body, then the face and hands holding the fish. Pin the back body pieces to the front and machine stitch round, leaving the base open.

Stitch the leg seam in the centre of the body, from the waistband to the feet. To complete, glue the features on to the face.

### 2. Hula Girl

Trace off the pattern for the Hula Girl. Cut out front body, top back body, lower back body and hands in brown felt, hair pieces in black felt, skirt pieces in green felt and the flowers, bracelets and features in scraps of felt.

Snip across the green skirt pieces to

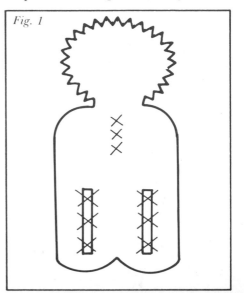

*Fig. 1*

# Trace patterns for finger puppets

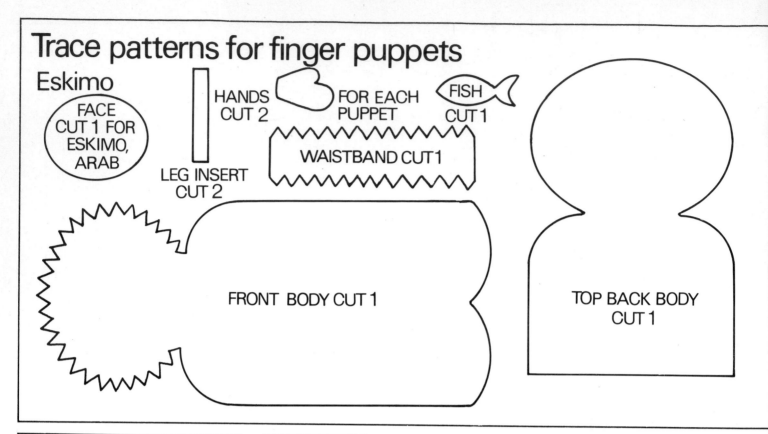

## Eskimo

FACE CUT 1 FOR ESKIMO, ARAB

HANDS CUT 2

FOR EACH PUPPET

FISH CUT 1

LEG INSERT CUT 2

WAISTBAND CUT 1

FRONT BODY CUT 1

TOP BACK BODY CUT 1

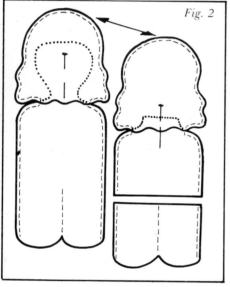

*Fig. 2*

*Fig. 3*

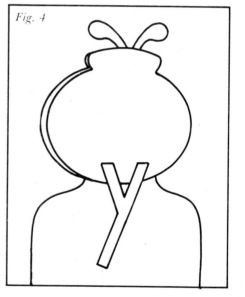

*Fig. 4*

form grass skirt, and snip the flowers to form petals. Pin one hair piece to the front body (Fig.2) and one hair piece to the top back body. Pin the top back and lower back body to the front body and machine round, leaving the base open.

Glue the face to the hair. Work the leg seam in the same position as the Eskimo. Glue on the flowers, skirt pieces, hands and add the features to the face.

## 3. Arab

Trace off the pattern for the Arab. Cut out front body, top back and lower back body in purple felt, both head-dresses and cuff decorations in yellow felt, the face and hands in beige felt, the cuffs and feet in cream felt, the headband and waistband and features in scraps of felt.

Glue the headband to the front head-dress, then the front head-dress to the face, and the base of the front head-dress and face to the top of the front body (Fig.3).

Pin the back head-dress, the top and lower back body to the front body, and machine stitch round, leaving the base open.

Stitch the leg seam. Attach the feet, cuffs, hands, cut decorations and the features for the face.

## 4. Geisha Girl

Trace off the pattern for the Geisha girl. Cut out front, top back and lower back body pieces in turquoise felt, face, hands and feet in cream felt, head pieces and sandals in black felt and hair pins, flowers, neckline, belt-tie, decorations and features in scraps of felt.

Glue the two head pieces together enclosing the hair pins. Glue the kimono neckline to the front head and front body (Fig.4) the face to the head over the neckline and the sandals to the feet and the feet to the body. Machine stitch the front and back bodies together, leaving the base open, and stitch the leg seam. Glue on the belt and decoration, hands, cuffs, flowers and features for the face.

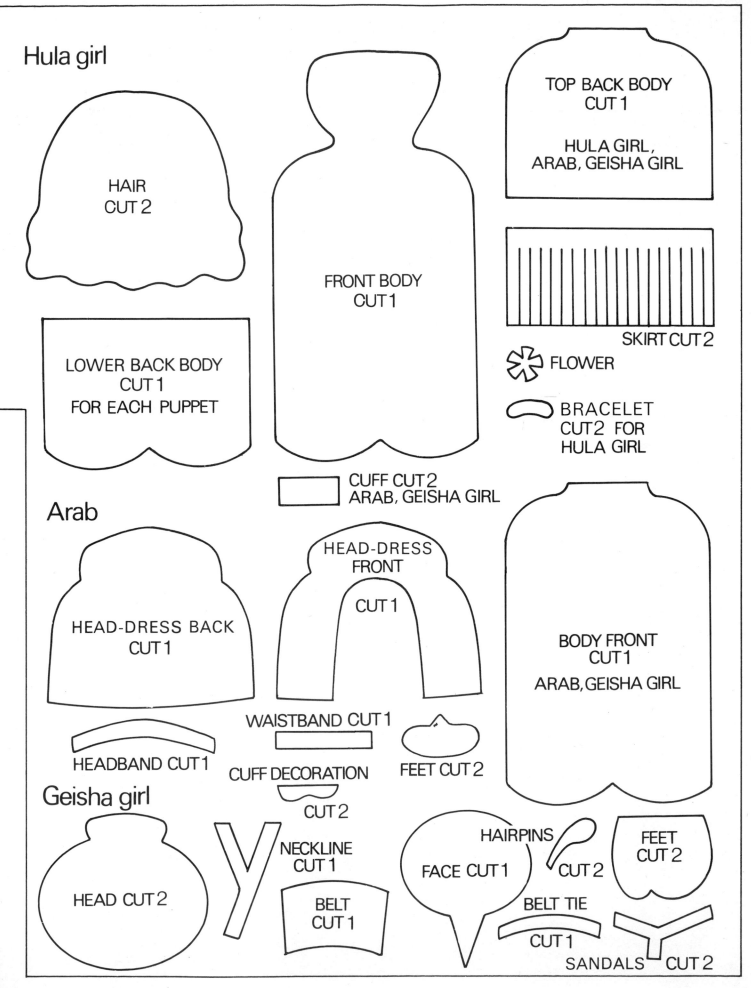

Hula girl

HAIR
CUT 2

FRONT BODY
CUT 1

TOP BACK BODY
CUT 1

HULA GIRL,
ARAB, GEISHA GIRL

SKIRT CUT 2

✳ FLOWER

◗ BRACELET
CUT 2 FOR
HULA GIRL

LOWER BACK BODY
CUT 1
FOR EACH PUPPET

CUFF CUT 2
ARAB, GEISHA GIRL

Arab

HEAD-DRESS
FRONT

CUT 1

HEAD-DRESS BACK
CUT 1

BODY FRONT
CUT 1

ARAB, GEISHA GIRL

WAISTBAND CUT 1

HEADBAND CUT 1

CUFF DECORATION

FEET CUT 2

CUT 2

Geisha girl

HEAD CUT 2

NECKLINE
CUT 1

HAIRPINS

FACE CUT 1

CUT 2

FEET
CUT 2

BELT
CUT 1

BELT TIE

CUT 1

SANDALS    CUT 2

# Dolls' house

Transform four square biscuit [cookie] tins into a pair of elegant Georgian town houses. The front of the houses can be folded back to reveal four floors of rooms, which can be filled with simple furniture ingeniously made from household items, suggestions for which are given below.

## You will need:

- 1.8m *(2yd)* of 0.6cm *($\frac{1}{4}$in)* quarter round dowelling
- 46cm *(18in)* of 1.3cm *($\frac{1}{2}$in)* dowelling
- four 23cm *(9in)* square biscuit [cookie] or cake tins
- 2 empty cotton reels [thread spools]
- thick cardboard
- epoxy resin; glue suitable for fabric
- fine string; fine wire
- piece of felt 23cm x 69cm *(9in x 27in)*
- 57cm *($\frac{5}{8}$yd)* tweed fabric
- 57cm *($\frac{5}{8}$yd)* canvas
- 57cm *($\frac{5}{8}$yd)* lining fabric
- 23cm *($\frac{1}{4}$yd)* of 5cm *(2in)* wide black Cluny lace
- 1.4m *(1$\frac{1}{2}$yd)* narrow black lace
- 57cm *($\frac{5}{8}$yd)* white guipure lace
- approximately 24 flower-shaped sequins and tiny beads
- 3.2m *(3$\frac{1}{2}$yd)* of 1.5cm *($\frac{5}{8}$in)* wide furnishing braid
- two black beads
- scraps of plastic-covered adhesive paper [contact paper], wrapping paper, felt, velvet etc., for interior decoration
- small pieces of felt for doorsteps and window boxes
- black and white soft stranded embroidery thread
- invisible or transparent thread

## To make the house front

Draw up the graph pattern onto stiff paper. The dotted lines indicate the position of the balcony and railings. Cut out the twelve windows and the two fan lights over the doors, and pin them in position on the canvas. Tack [baste] around the edges of the windows and mark their positions lightly with a ball point pen. Remove the paper patterns.

Cut a piece of net for each window, allowing an extra 3.8cm *(1$\frac{1}{2}$in)* all round, and tack [baste] in position over the windows.

Using white thread, work a straight machine stitch around each window, and then work a close satin stitch over this, using a wide setting on the machine. Alternatively, work two more rows of straight stitching close to the first. Carefully cut away the canvas windows from the back of the net, and darn any accidental snips with invisible or transparent thread. Mark the lines dividing the window panes and the fan lights with running stitch, using soft white embroidery thread, as shown in the illustration. The window boxes on the top floor are formed in the same way, using black embroidery thread.

Cut six felt strips 2cm *($\frac{3}{4}$in)* wide for the other window boxes, and either machine stitch or sew neatly in place by hand, leaving the top edges open. Sew the sequins in position around the window boxes and attach a small bead to the centre of each. Alternatively, cut small circles of felt to form the flowers. Cut the white guipure lace into ten 5cm *(2in)* strips, and sew in position over the windows, as shown, to form the window headings.

The doors are cut from felt, and stitched in position on the canvas using a close zig-zag stitch. Alternatively, sew them in place neatly by hand.

The door panels are sewn by machine using black thread.

Trace and cut out the doorsteps from white felt, and mark the dotted line with straight machine stitching, using black thread. Embroider a circle or horseshoe shape in satin stitch on each door, to form the door knockers, and attach the black threads to form the handles.

### The balcony and railings

Trace off the balcony roof and cut out from felt. Scallop the lower edge, and stitch in place as shown, leaving the scallops free. The markings are in

straight machine stitch, using black thread.

The ground-floor railings are formed by stitching the narrow black lace in a curve, following the dotted line on the graph. Make straight railings as shown, either in stem stitch or back stitch, using black embroidery thread, or work them on the machine.

The three balcony pillars are each made from two 15cm *(6in)* lengths of narrow black lace, stitched side by side. Sew the straight edges of the lace to the outside of the pillars, and oversew [overcast] the top edges of the pillars under the balcony roof. In between the bases of the pillars stitch two pieces of the wide black lace. Press the work well on the wrong side.

## To finish

Draw the graph pattern onto the lining fabric.

Draw two diagonal lines across each window and cut (Fig.1a). Press back the triangles (Fig.1b) and trim them off to 1.3cm *($\frac{1}{2}$in)* (Fig.1c).

Make sure before pressing the lining that the windows correspond exactly to those on the canvas fronts.

Slip stitch the lining to the canvas around each window.

Measure the canvas to exactly 46cm *(18in)* square, and press the excess fabric at each side to the back. Trim the canvas only to 2.5cm *(1in)* all round. Trim and turn in the sides of the lining, and slip stitch to the canvas.

Leave about 7.5cm *(3in)* surplus canvas and lining at the top of the work to attach later to the top of the house. Turn in the lower edge to the wrong side to make a channel for the 1.3cm *($\frac{1}{2}$in)* size dowel. Stitch in place and insert the dowel.

## To complete the house

Decorate the inside of each tin to represent wallpaper, using odd pieces of plastic-covered adhesive paper [contact paper] and fabric, remembering that each tin is divided into two rooms by a horizontal partition.

On the front edges of the tins, trim the paper to 1.3cm *($\frac{1}{2}$in)*, so the edges may be covered later.

### Ceilings and floors

Cut eight pieces of cardboard, each 23cm *(9in)* long and the depth of the tins, to form the divisions.

Cut sixteen pieces of quarter round dowelling to the depth of the tins in length. Either paint or stick paper to one side of each piece of cardboard, to form the ceilings. Apply glue to three

edges of the wrong side of each piece of cardboard, and press four into position at the top of each tin, and stick the other four in position to divide each tin into two floors. Paint the lengths of dowelling, two for each ceiling, and apply glue to the straight edges. Stick in place on either side under each ceiling to give extra support, and to form the coving [molding].

Cut the pieces of fabric to size and stick in place to from the carpets.

If desired, the top floor can be divided in two vertically by a piece of stiff cardboard or plywood, to give two smaller rooms, as shown.

### To assemble

Mix the epoxy resin according to the instructions and glue the sides of the four tins together, to form a unit 46cm *(18in)* square. Tie fine string firmly around the outside of the unit to hold it together, and leave it to dry. Leave the string in place when the resin has dried, to give added strength to the unit. Cut two 50cm *(20in)* lengths of furnishing braid and glue

them centrally across the front of the unit, from top to bottom and from side to side, leaving an extra 2.5cm *(1in)* at each end. Stick braid all round the outside edge of the houses, so that it projects for approximately 0.6cm *($\frac{1}{4}$in)*. Attach the house front to the main unit by sticking the upper edge to the top of the tins with plenty of glue. Tie another piece of string tightly around the unit, 1.3cm *($\frac{1}{2}$in)* from the front edge, to ensure the front of the house is fixed securely in place.

### Roof and outside of houses

Cut two lengths of tweed, each 0.9m *(35in)* long, and the depth of the tins plus 5cm *(2in)*. Join the short edges together, taking a 1.3cm *($\frac{1}{2}$in)* seam, and press a 2.5cm *(1in)* turning [hem] along both sides of the long edges.

Apply glue to the sides of the tins, paying special attention to the braided front edges. Press the tweed in place, covering the top, bottom and sides of the tins, so that the raw edges meet at a lower corner. Overlap the ends, trim and sew in place neatly.

Cut a second piece of tweed 48.5cm (19in) square, and oversew [overcast] it to the back edges of the side coverings, turning in any surplus by approximately 1.3cm (½in) as you work.

Cut two pieces of cardboard for the roof, each 25cm (10in) long, and the depth of the tins plus 1.3cm (½in).

Cut two pieces of tweed to the same size as cardboard pieces plus 1.3cm (½in) all round. Stick the tweed to them, first pressing the extra fabric to the inside.

Apply felt to the other sides of the pieces of cardboard, and oversew [overcast] the two fabrics together around the edges.

Sew two short ends of cardboard pieces together. Stick a 0.6cm (¼in) wide strip of felt to cover the seam. Cut a strip of felt 50cm by 2.5cm (20in by 1in), scallop one long edge and sew it to the covered cards so that the scallops hang down.

Take the two empty cotton reels [spools] and cover them with felt to match the roof. Stick the reels [spools] on their sides in the centre of the house tops, one at the front and one at the back.

Stick the centre of the roof on top of the reels [spools] and apply adhesive to each short end of the house top. Stick the roof down at each end, and then sew a few stitches at each end for extra strength.

## Ideas for making furniture

**Chairs.** A handsome three piece suite can be simply made from pieces of foam 2.5cm (1in) thick, covered in satin or velvet [velveteen] ribbon. To make the chairs, cut cubes 2.5cm (1in) square, and for the settee cut a piece of foam 2.5cm x 6.5cm (1in x 2½in). Add arms and backs cut from thin cardboard. Cover the pieces separately by gluing on the fabric, and assemble them when dry. Chicken wishbones can be made into chairs, with a matchstick forming the third leg. First immerse the bone in bleach to whiten. Cover a triangle of cardboard and stick it in between the three legs so that the wishbone curves backwards, forming the arms and front legs. A capacious armchair can be made from one section of an egg carton, filled with a felt cushion.

Covered buttons, mounted on other buttons, with a length of dowelling between them, make perfect one-legged stools.

**Tables.** An effective dressing table can be made from a piece cut from a coloured polystyrene egg carton, mounted on a matchbox, and decorated with a gathered lace skirt. Add a polystyrene back, and stick a piece of silver foil in position as a looking glass. Other simple tables may be made from jar lids or pieces of cardboard with dowelling legs; or mount a circle of plastic or glass on a small cosmetic pot or cotton reel.

**Beds.** Use covered matchboxes, and add bedheads made from padded and covered cardboard.

A rocking cradle can be made from a matchbox with curved cardboard rockers.

**Cupboards.** Cover matchboxes and stick on beads for handles.

**Fireplace.** Cover two matchboxes with suitable paper and lay them on their long sides with a space in between. Cut a strip of cardboard for the mantel, then cut a piece of cardboard to form the hearth and add coloured tissue paper to represent flames.

**Accessories.** Bathroom equipment is difficult to simulate and is best bought. Exotic postage stamps, suitably mounted, make ideal pictures for the walls. A circular brooch with a piece of foil stuck to the centre, becomes a wall mirror, and other mirrors can be made from large silver sequins with beads stuck all round them, mounted on a piece of cardboard.

Use tiny rolls of cardboard to form flower vases, filled with artificial flowers from cake decorations.

Rugs may be made from scraps of embroidered ribbon or fur fabric.

Linen buttons, marked with felt tip pens, make perfect plates, and in the kitchen, a sink unit can be made from a large matchbox cut in half lengthways, with a bottle top set in it for the sink.

For the nursery, a rocking horse can be created from pipe cleaners wound round with wool [yarn] and shaped into a horse. Mount it on a rocker made from a piece of cardboard which has first been curved by wetting and rolling around a bottle to dry.

Shelves can be created by sticking pieces of quarter round dowelling to the walls, and tiny shells, buttons and glass balls make suitable ornaments.

Many other items of simple furniture and decoration can be made from odd pieces of fabric and household materials, and this model with its four floors of rooms provides ample scope for innovation and imagination.

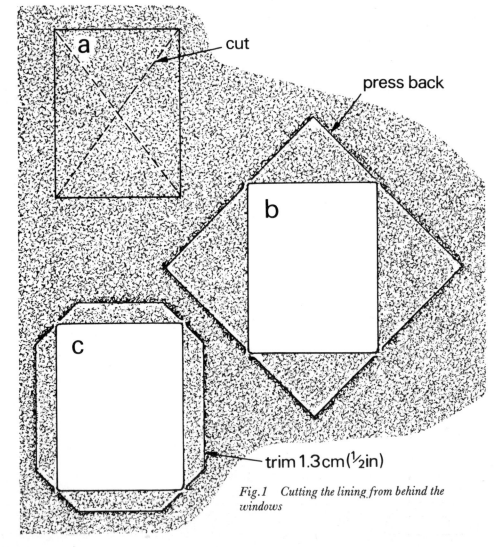

*Fig.1 Cutting the lining from behind the windows*

# Graph pattern for front of dolls' house

Each square=2.5cm (1in) sq

# Canvas tunnel

Here is a super present for children who enjoy playing outside – a canvas tunnel brightened with colourful clouds and rainbows! The tunnel will be 2.75m (9ft) long and 66cm (26in) in diameter.

## You will need:

☐ 6.40m (7yd) of 90cm (36in) wide canvas
☐ matching heavy-weight thread
☐ 5.50m (6yd) of cotton [bias] binding 2.5cm (1in) wide
☐ 0.45m ($\frac{1}{2}$yd) of net for window panes
☐ 20m (22yd) of strong wire
☐ 0.9m (1yd) white felt 90cm (36in) wide
☐ rectangles of felt in seven colours for rainbow, each 38cm x 15cm (15in x 6in)
☐ cotton wool [absorbent cotton]

## To make the tunnel

Measure the fabric into three sections along its length and mark lightly with pencil. Cut across the fabric from selvedge to selvedge on these marks.
Using graph paper and following the pattern given, draw the cloud, the window and the rainbow pattern pieces to scale.
Cut out the pattern pieces.
One square =2.5cm (1in) square.
An allowance of 1.5cm ($\frac{5}{8}$in) has been made on the seams of the play tunnel and 0.6cm ($\frac{1}{4}$in) has been allowed on the pieces for the rainbow.
From the white felt cut out two windows and two clouds. Cut out the pieces for two rainbows from the coloured felts. Fold the net in half and place the felt windows on top of net. Pin into place and cut out the net around the outer edge of the windows.

## Making up

With right sides and selvedges matching tack [baste] and stitch the three tunnel sections together. Press seams open.
On the wrong side, tack [baste] the binding over the seams and stitch close to each edge. Tack [baste] and stitch a binding in the same way halfway between each section. Press 1.5cm ($\frac{5}{8}$in) to the wrong side on each end of the tunnel. Tack [baste] and stitch as close

to the selvedge as possible, starting and finishing 4cm (1$\frac{1}{2}$in) from each edge.
Tack [baste] and stitch the net behind the white felt windows around the cut-out sections using a small zig-zag stitch or two rows of straight stitches worked close together.
Join each section of the rainbow with a small zig-zag stitch or top stitching.
Pin and tack [baste] the rainbow into position on one side of the tunnel near the end. Place the window over the narrow end of the rainbow and the cloud over the other end. Tack [baste] and stitch around the window with two rows of straight stitching 0.6cm ($\frac{1}{4}$in) from the edge. Stitch on the rainbow and cloud the same distance from the edge as the window. Using sharp scissors and taking care not to cut the net trim away the blue canvas behind each window pane.
Repeat the decoration on the other side of the tunnel on the opposite end.

## To support the tunnel

With right sides together, tack [baste] and stitch the long sides of the canvas together turning in the ends of the binding. Neaten seam and press open.
Insert wire into each binding and into each end seam of the tunnel. Cut each length of wire to pass three times round inside each binding.
Bind all ends of the wire together with strong thread and pad with cotton wool [absorbent cotton] to prevent sharp ends protruding.
Place binding over the ends of the wire and hem stitch into place on the bottom seam.
Insert two eyelets into the top of the tunnel at each end. Rope threaded through these eyelets is used to support the tunnel. For extra strength, a bamboo cane or long cardboard tube can be hung through the rope loops. Before children play check that tunnel is secure.

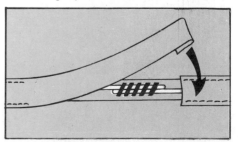

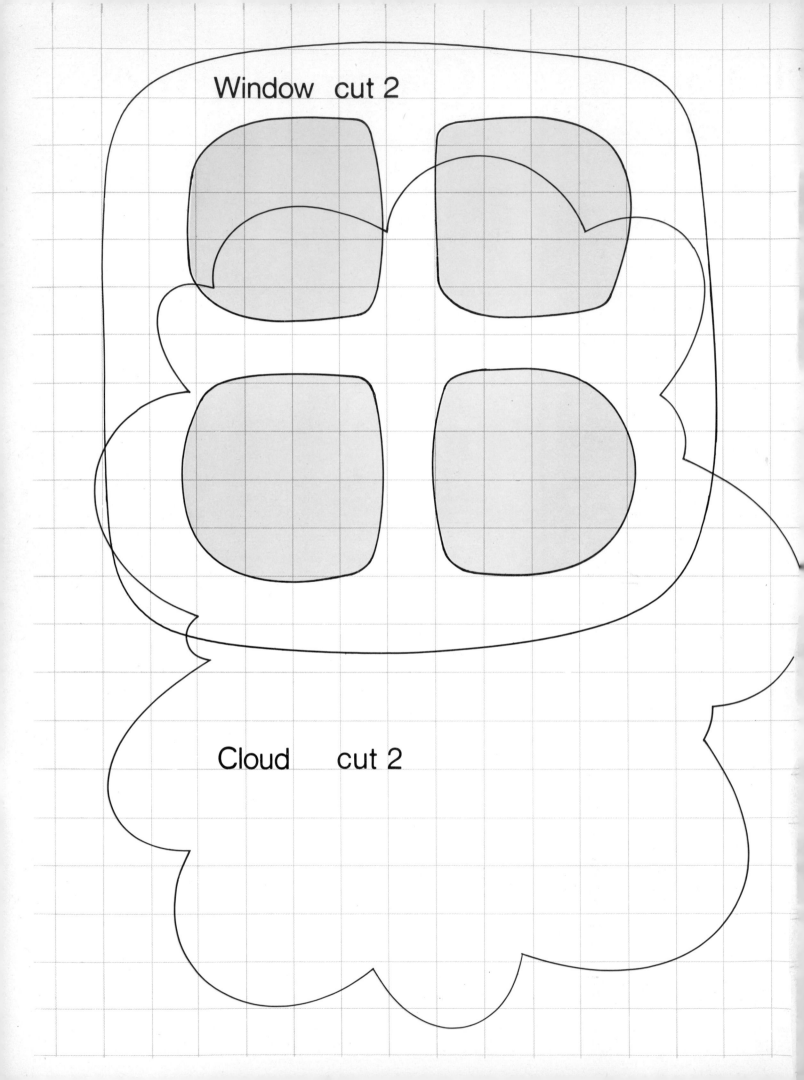

Window  cut 2

Cloud    cut 2

# Graph pattern for canvas tunnel

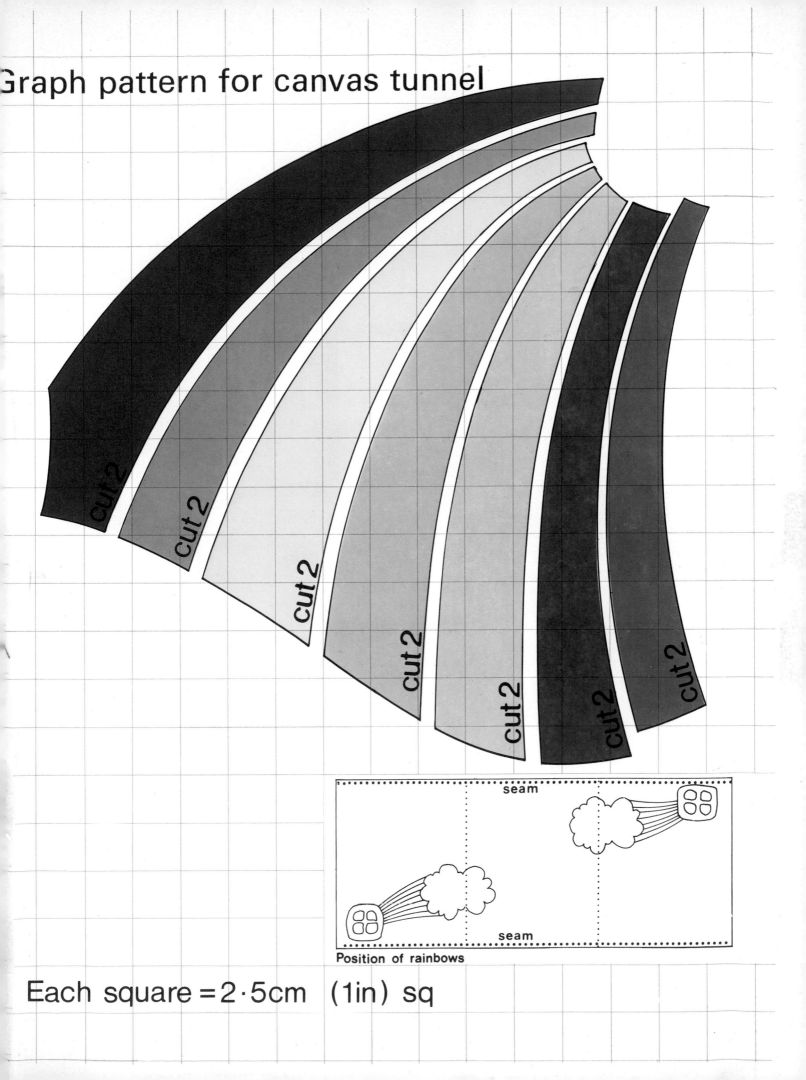

cut 2

cut 2

cut 2

cut 2

cut 2

cut 2

cut 2

cut 2

seam

seam

**Position of rainbows**

Each square = 2·5cm (1in) sq

# Playhouse

This decorative playhouse is a very unusual gift and an ideal hideaway for children.

**Materials you will need for the basic house to fit a table measuring approximately 122cm _(48in)_ long, 73.5cm _(29in)_ wide and 79cm _(31in)_ high.**

## Walls

☐ unbleached calico [heavy unbleached muslin], the amount to be calculated as follows:–

side wall: the height of table+5cm _(2in)_ x width of table+5cm _(2in)_

back wall: the height of table+5cm _(2in)_ x length of table+28cm _(11in)_ for underwrap at door

front wall: the height of table+5cm _(2in)_ x length of table+15cm _(6in)_

## Door

☐ piece of red sailcloth to fit height of table+5cm _(2in)_ x width of table −20cm _(8in)_

## Window measuring 36cm by 34cm _(14in by 13½in)_

☐ piece of lace curtain net measuring slightly larger than window size
☐ 1.5m _(1½yd)_ black petersham [grosgrain] ribbon, 1.5cm _(⅝in)_ wide
☐ 2 pieces red sailcloth for shutters, 36cm by 19cm _(14in by 7½in)_
☐ 2 pieces of gingham, 42cm by 24cm _(16½in by 9½in)_

## Roof

☐ piece of blue cotton fabric to fit width of table+5cm _(2in)_ x length of table+5cm _(2in)_
☐ sewing thread in appropriate colours

**Materials you will need to decorate the house:**

## Bricks

☐ postcard to use as template
☐ tan sewing thread

## Flowers

☐ for each flower:– 18cm _(7in)_ square of felt and scraps in contrasting colours
☐ scraps of green felt for stems and leaves
☐ ends of embroidery thread

## Potted shrubs

☐ large shrub: a piece of green felt 50cm by 23cm _(20in by 9in)_; piece of brown felt 17cm by 13cm _(7in by 5½in)_
☐ small shrub: a piece of green felt 30cm by 18cm _(12in by 7in)_; piece of brown felt 9cm by 4cm _(3½in by 2in)_

## Bird house

☐ 18cm _(7in)_ square of navy felt
☐ 0.4m _(½yd)_ black petersham [grosgrain] ribbon, 2cm _(¾in)_ wide

## Birds

☐ scraps of red and mauve felt

## Ladybirds

☐ scraps of red and black felt

## Door knocker, letter box and handle

☐ 20.5cm _(8in)_ square of black felt

## Apple tree

☐ 2.75m _(3yd)_ brown petersham [grosgrain] ribbon, 2.5cm _(1in)_ wide
☐ 1.5m _(1¾yd)_ brown petersham [grosgrain] ribbon, 1.5cm _(⅝in)_ wide
☐ large quantity of scrap felt in 2 shades of green for leaves
☐ 30.5cm _(12in)_ square of red felt for apples
☐ sewing threads in appropriate colours

## Choosing a suitable table

The most important requirement for the playhouse is a table of the very simplest type – basically a slab of wood with a leg at each corner. Tables with struts near the floor are unsuitable as they would make play very difficult. The table should be big enough to let at least two children be in residence at a time.

If you are using a table of very different proportions to the one illustrated, you will need to alter the shapes of the door and window accordingly and possibly change the position of the decorations slightly. It may be helpful to make a scale drawing before you begin, showing not only the proportions of each item but also the colour scheme that you intend to use.

# Graph pattern for playhouse decorations

Each square=2.5cm(1in)sq

## To make the playhouse

Calculate the measurements of the walls, door and roof according to the size of the table. Cut the pieces out from the appropriate fabric.

Indicate the corner folds in the long back and front walls with a line of tacking [basting] stitches. Pin, tack [baste] and machine stitch the side wall to the back and front walls, making machine fell seams for a neat finish.

Stitch one side edge of the door to the front wall, leaving the other edge of the door free.

Turn under a hem on the side edge of the door, on the side edge of the back wall and all round the bottom of the house.

Stitch the roof to the walls and door, overlapping the open side of the door with the back wall for about 12.5cm *(5in)*. Cut out a black felt knocker, a letter box and a door knob and machine stitch in place on the door.

**Bricks.** Using a postcard as a template, mark round the four sides with a sharp pencil, rounding off at the corners. Machine stitch three times round the shape, making the lines slightly irregular for a softer effect. Place bricks at random on all the walls.

**Window.** Draw the shape of the window in pencil on the right side of the fabric. Stay stitch the corners to strengthen them. Cut out the centre area of the window to within 1cm *(⅜in)* of the pencil line. Slash the corners up to the stay stitching. Fold the seam allowance to the right side along the pencil line.

Lay the house flat on a large table with the right side facing upwards. Place the curtain net over the hole, pin and tack [baste] firmly in place.

**Window frame.** Make the centre

cross first, using the petersham [grosgrain] ribbon. Then finish off the top and bottom edges, covering the raw edges of the curtain net.

**Shutters.** Turn under the edges of the sailcloth, then pin, tack [baste] and machine in place.

**Curtains.** Turn under a small hem all round the curtain pieces. Machine stitch to the top of the window inside the house.

**The apple tree.** Lay the back wall face up on a flat surface, so that the whole area can be seen at a glance. Begin by pinning on the most important branches, making neat folds at the corners and folding under the ends of the branches. Fill in the gaps with small branches, tucking the lower ends under the main branches.

When stitching the branches, begin with the ones whose ends will be hidden under other branches. The ribbon which forms the trunks should be sewn down last of all.

Cut out approximately 50 leaves, some dark green, some light green. Pin and stitch in place in a pleasing arrangement.

Cut out approximately 17 apples, pin and stitch in place.

**Flowers.** For the heads, cut circles about 14cm *(5½in)* in diameter or flower shapes from different coloured felts.

Cut smaller circles of felt for the centres. Stitch the stems and leaves in place

around the walls and top each stem with a flower head held in place and decorated with different embroidery stitches. Blanket stitch, herringbone stitch, French knots and back stitch are simple and pretty.

**The birds and birdhouse.** Cut out the birdhouse from the navy felt and stitch in place. A length of petersham [grosgrain] ribbon forms the post.

The birds are decorated and attached to the top of the birdhouse in a similar way to the flowers. Work blanket stitch around the body, stem stitch around the neck and wings.

**The shrubs and ladybirds.** Cut out a large and a small shrub and stitch in place. To make a ladybird, cut a black felt circle for the body, stitch red felt wings over this and decorate with black spots.

### Other ideas for playhouses

Fabric houses can be adapted to fit all kinds of play situations and require only simple materials and a little imagination. A pair of old blue sheets decorated with clouds, birds, a bright yellow sun and a rainbow would make a delightful house in the sky. Yellow sheets could be covered with pretty shells, fish and a mermaid or two and green ribbon attached as a seaweed door curtain to make an underwater house. A jungle house surrounded by wild animals for budding Tarzans would also be fun.

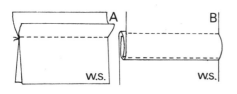

*To work a machine fell seam, stitch along the fitting line, trim one raw edge to 0·3cm (⅛in), turn in the wider raw edge around the narrow one and edge stitch close to the folded edge*

▲ *The apple tree on the back wall*　　　*Making up the walls and door* ▼

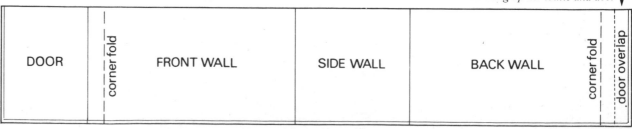

# Hobby horse

This hobby horse, which looks marvellous in brightly coloured fabric, will keep a little boy or girl happy for hours.

## You will need:

☐ 0.7m (¾yd) of 90cm (36in) wide fabric
☐ graph paper for making the pattern
☐ matching thread
☐ 1 x 25grm (1oz) ball of knitting wool [yarn] for mane
☐ 15cm (6in) square of yellow felt
☐ 2 x 25cm (10in) squares of brown felt
☐ 1.85m (2yd) decorative braid for reins
☐ 2 small bells
☐ kapok or foam rubber chips
☐ 1 broom handle, 2.5cm (1in) in diameter
☐ strong glue

## To make the hobby horse

Using graph paper draw the ear, head, and gusset pieces to scale. One square = 2.5cm square (1in square). An allowance of 1.5cm (⅝in) has been made on seams for the head, gusset and ears. Mark dots, lines and positions for eyes. Trace the pattern for the eye, and nostril from eye pupil piece. Cut out pattern pieces.
Fold the fabric in half with the selvedges together. Place on the three main pattern pieces, with the gusset on the fold. Make sure that the grain line on the pattern lies on the straight grain of the fabric. Pin into place and cut out. From yellow felt, cut out the ear piece twice and each of the eye pieces twice.
From brown felt cut out the neck decoration once, the rein decoration twice, and the nostril piece twice and the eye piece twice.
Transfer all markings from the pattern pieces to the fabric.

## To make up the head

Tack [baste] and top-stitch the yellow pupil to the brown eye piece where indicated. Using a small zig-zag stitch or close buttonhole stitch, sew the yellow eyelid to the brow eye piece where marked. Catch-stitch eyes to head pieces in the positions indicated.
With right sides together and matching dots, tack [baste] and stitch the gusset to the head pieces, easing carefully on curves (Fig.1).
Tack [baste] and stitch the back neck seam and the front neck seam from the point of gusset to neck edge (Fig 2). Fasten off securely. Trim turnings, clip curves and turn through to the right side. Work a row of gathers around

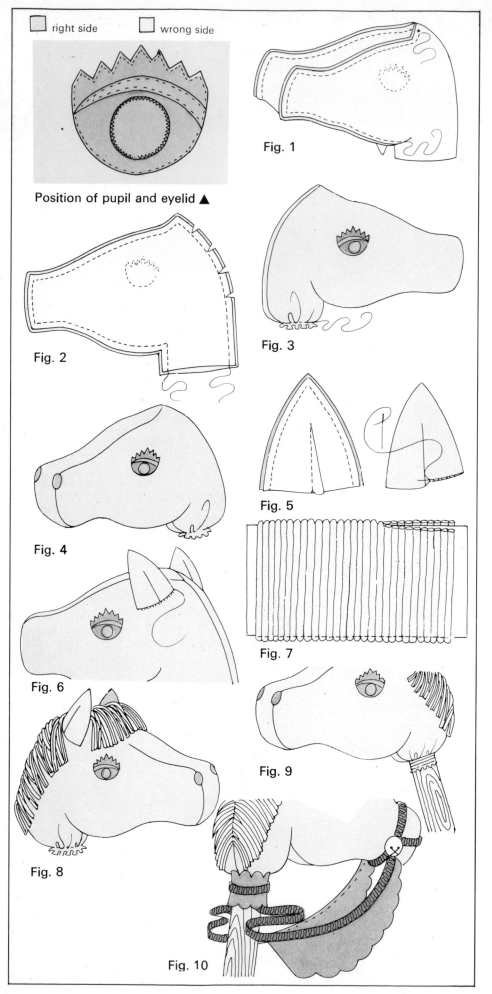

right side      wrong side

Position of pupil and eyelid ▲

Fig. 1

Fig. 2

Fig. 3

Fig. 4

Fig. 5

Fig. 6

Fig. 7

Fig. 8

Fig. 9

Fig. 10

neck, 0.6cm (¼in) from the edge.

Stuff head carefully with kapok, making sure it is firmly and evenly packed. Pull up gathers round neck and secure to prevent the kapok from escaping (Fig.3). Catch-stitch nostrils to the front of nose, positioning them on top curve (Fig.4).

**Ears.** With right sides together tack [baste] and stitch the darts on outer ear and yellow felt ears. Press to one side. With right sides together tack [baste] and stitch the ears on the seam line. Make a small hem on the bottom edge of each ear and slip-stitch (Fig.5).

Position the ears of either side of the head, close to the gusset seam. Stitch firmly into place, making sure that the ears are upright (Fig.6).

**To complete the horse**

**Mane.** Wind the wool [yarn] evenly round a piece of cardboard 10cm (4in) wide and 20.5cm (8in) long. Using matching thread, work a line of back stitches through wool [yarn] at one edge of the cardboard to hold the wool [yarn] together. Cut through loops on other edge (Fig. 7). Position the mane down the back neck seam, starting from behind the ears. Using wool [yarn], stitch into position covering the back stitches.

Make a front fringe in the same way to measure 7.5cm (3in) and attach to the head with stitching running from one ear to the other ear. Make sure that the fringe and mane meet. Fold the fringe forward between the ears (Fig.8).

**Handle.** Carefully open the neck gathers and push the broom handle as far as possible into the head. Pack kapok around the broom handle and pull up the gathers.

Stick the turnings [seam allowance] on the neck to the broom handle with strong glue and bind the head on to the handle with several strands of thread (Fig.9).

**Reins.** Cut the braid into three lengths: one piece for neck decoration 10cm (4in) long; one piece for the nose-band 42cm (16½in) long; and the remainder for the reins.

Tack [baste] and stitch the braid to the neck decoration. Find the centre of the reins and stitch the rein decoration onto the braid 14cm (5½in) either side of this point. Pin nose band on to horse's nose and join the ends under the chin. Pin reins on to head with centre of rein in centre of mouth. Stitch the reins to the nose and where they cross attach bells.

Glue the ends of the reins to the neck and cover these by sticking the neck decoration over all raw edges. Neatly stitch the two ends together (Fig.10).

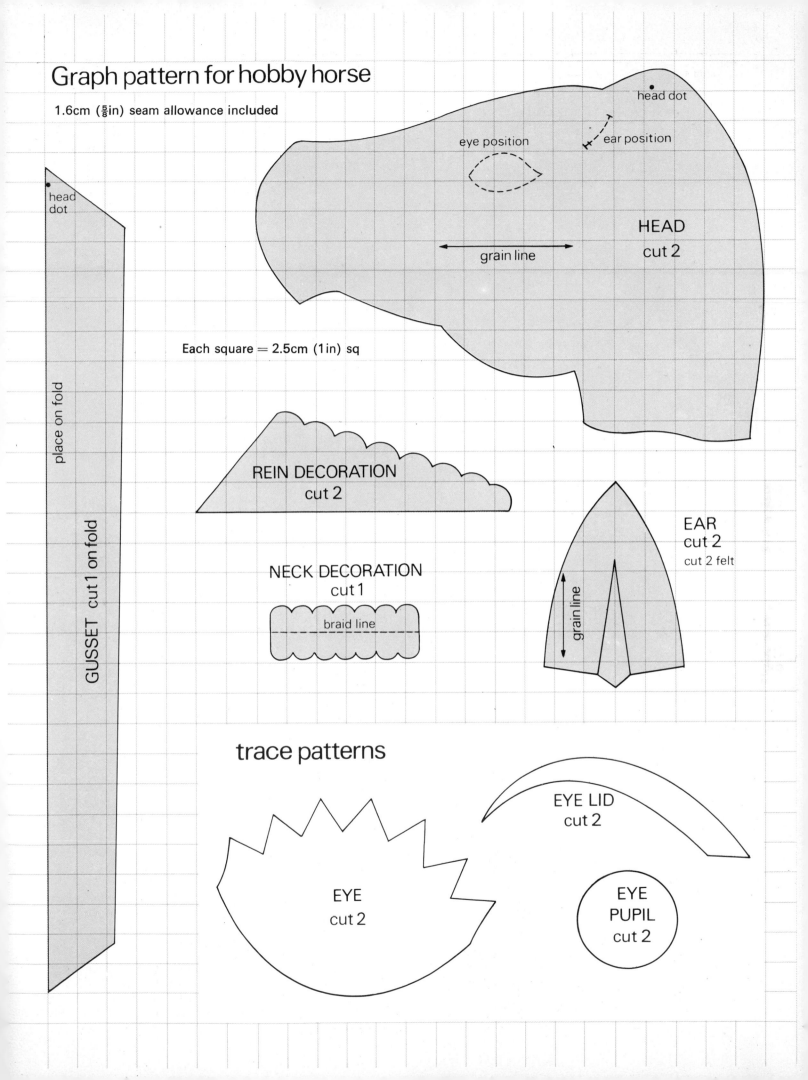

# Graph pattern for hobby horse

1.6cm (⅝in) seam allowance included

head dot

eye position

ear position

head dot

HEAD
cut 2

Each square = 2.5cm (1in) sq

grain line

place on fold

GUSSET cut 1 on fold

REIN DECORATION
cut 2

NECK DECORATION
cut 1

braid line

EAR
cut 2
cut 2 felt

grain line

trace patterns

EYE LID
cut 2

EYE
cut 2

EYE
PUPIL
cut 2

# A high-flying kite

What better way to spend a windy Sunday afternoon than flying a kite in the park or in the country. Our black-and-white ghost looks suitably spooky high up in the sky. An owl, a butterfly or an exotic bird are more colourful alternatives.

## To make the ghost kite

### You will need:

- [ ] two 91.5cm *(3ft)* green garden canes or similar 'springy' sticks
- [ ] thin but strong black paper 51cm by 76cm *(20in by 30in)*
- [ ] thin white paper 43cm by 56cm *(17in by 22in)*
- [ ] carpet thread or fine string
- [ ] coloured tissue paper
- [ ] clear glue
- [ ] clear adhesive tape [cellophane tape]
- [ ] 1 curtain ring
- [ ] reel of kite string
- [ ] sharp knife
- [ ] scissors
- [ ] black felt tip pen
- [ ] ruler
- [ ] pencil

### To make the kite frame

Cut the canes to length – one to 71cm *(28in)*, the other to 51cm *(20in)*. Measure and mark the exact centre of the shorter cane and mark the longer cane 23.6cm *(9¼in)* from one end.
Form the canes into a cross, joining them where they are marked. Bind them together with carpet thread, then glue over the thread to fix securely. Measure and mark 0.6cm *(¼in)* in from the end of each cane then, with a sharp knife, cut a very small notch at each of the four marks. Cut a 2.14m *(7ft)* length of thread. Find the centre of it and tie it to the top of the cross shape, using the notch to stop the thread from slipping out of place. Then take the right hand piece of thread and tie it to the right 'arm' of the cross at the notch. Do the same on the left side, and then tie both strings to the bottom of the cross. The string should not be at all slack. Glue all the knots. The string forms the outline of the kite's shape.

### To cover the kite

Place the kite frame on the reverse side

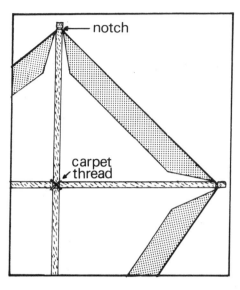

*Folding the paper on the kite frame*

of the black paper and draw around the outline of the string with a pencil. Remove the frame and straighten the lines with a ruler.
Cut out kite shape, allowing at least 2.5cm *(1in)* all round outside the pencil line. Stick adhesive [cellophane] tape over the pencil lines to strengthen paper when folded. Cut out a ghost shape from the white paper and draw on eyes and mouth with a black pen. Glue ghost onto front side of kite shape. Lay the frame onto the reverse side of the kite shape and fold the paper along the pencil lines over the string. Cut 'V' shapes at each corner so that the flaps lie flat, then glue the flaps down.

### The tail

Cut a length of thread at least twice the length of the kite. Cut pieces of tissue paper 15cm by 25.5cm *(6in by 10in)* and pleat them along the 25.5cm *(10in)* lengths. Twist them in the centre and tie them at 10cm *(4in)* intervals along the thread. When finished the tail should be at least 1½ times the length of the kite.
Make three tassels from strips of tissue paper 25.5cm by 1.3cm *(10in by ½in)*, tied in the centre and folded over. Tie one to each 'arm' of the kite and one to the bottom of the tail.

### The towing string

Cut two pieces of thread, one 84cm *(33in)* long and the other 63.5cm *(25in)* long. Loop the longer thread through the curtain ring as shown and then fix the ends of the thread to the top and bottom of the kite frame across the front of the kite. Slide the ring along the thread until it is about 29.5cm *(11½in)* from the top of the kite.

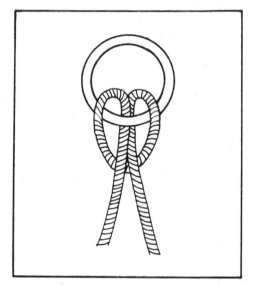

*Attaching the towing string to the curtain ring*

Attach the shorter string in the same way and fix the ends to the arms of the kite.
The curtain ring should be roughly in line with the point where the sticks cross when the string is held away from the kite. Fix the kite string to the curtain ring.

### Flying the kite

If only a short tail is made, a weight will be necessary on the bottom of the tail – this stops the kite from spinning and diving. Use one or two small coins and fix them on with adhesive [cellophane] tape. In a strong wind this may be needed even on a long tail.
It may also be necessary to alter the position of the curtain ring according to the wind.
Never wind the kite string around your hand when flying the kite as sudden gusts of wind could cut your hand. It is a good idea to have someone to hold the kite's tail when preparing to fly the kite to prevent it getting tangled with the kite line.

*Any of these colourful designs would look effective painted on a kite.*

**Other ideas for kites**

The owl, butterfly and bird designs could all be painted onto the kite cover with thinned acrylic paints before the cover is fixed to the kite frame, or done as a collage.

The kites may also be made from fabric which is much stronger than paper.

The ghost may be made from sheeting and the design painted on with black ink. Try also using a poster of a pop star or perhaps pretty wrapping paper instead of one of the designs shown here.

# Graph pattern for ghost shape
each square 2.5 cm (1 in) sq

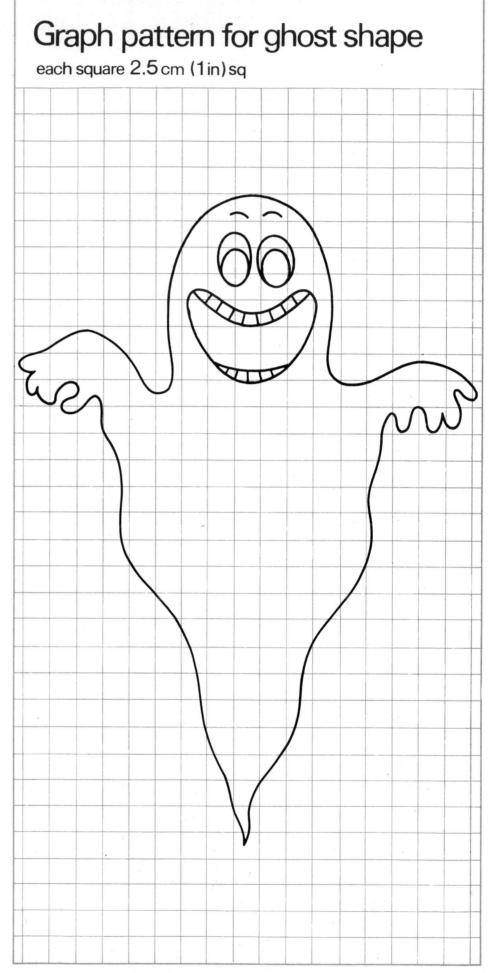

# Stitch library

The stitches shown are easily worked. Allow the threads to lie easily on the surface of the fabric. It should not be pulled out of shape by the stitch. To prevent threads knotting: with a woollen thread stitch in the direction of the natural lie of the wool. Run a hand along the thread. In one direction the hairs lie flatter than in the other. For stranded cotton: cut the length of thread, not more than 46cm *(18in)* for a trouble-free needleful. Divide at the centre for the number of strands required. You will find that they will separate easily without knotting.

## Back stitch

A very firm stitch worked by taking needle and thread back one stitch on side facing you, inserting needle just in front of preceding stitch.

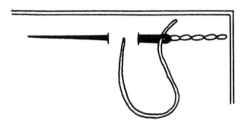

## Cross stitch

For an even appearance, work one row below another. The stitches should cross in the same direction throughout the work.

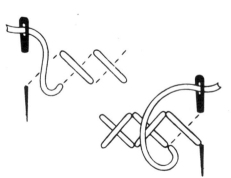

## Slip stitch

Holds the hem in position with very little stitching showing on the right side.

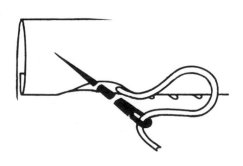

## French knot

To make a well-shaped knot, as the needle returns into the fabric, keep the thread taut.

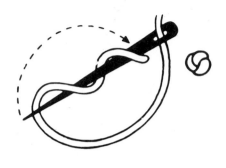

## Stem stitch

Use for straight and curved lines. Notice the position of the thread for left and right hand curves. Begin on the traced line and work inward when used to fill a shape.

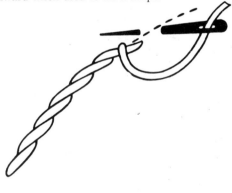

## Running stitch

Use the stitch as an outline, or in rows as filling stitch.

## Satin stitch

Most easily worked in a frame. The movements of the needle are simple. Hold the thread in position before inserting the needle. The stitches will lie smoothly side by side. For a raised effect, first pad with running stitches.

## Herringbone stitch (closed)

The movements of the needle are the same as for open herringbone stitch, but the needle comes out close to the previous stitch.

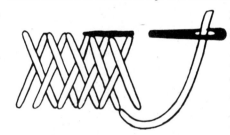

## Chain stitch

The needle returns to the place where it came out. The thread loops under it. Chain stitch may be worked in straight or curved lines. Use it in circles or rows to fill a shape. When used as a filling, begin at the outer edge and work inward.